"*High-Risk Homosexual* is a keen and tender exploration of queer identity, masculinity, and belonging. From the cockfighting ring in Nicaragua, where he was taken by his uncles to learn how to be a man, to Pulse nightclub in Orlando, where he witnesses freedom and joy on the dance floor, Edgar Gomez writes with honesty and humor about the difficulty of straddling boundaries and the courage of finding oneself. This book signals the arrival of a major new talent."

> —Laila Lalami, author of *Conditional Citizens: On Belonging in America* and *The Other Americans*

"*High-Risk Homosexual* is like a delicious cocktail: sharp, nuanced, sweet, and tender when the bite must be tempered. Edgar Gomez writes with the magnetic candor that flourishes at gay bars, with as much style as all the queens at DragCon, with observant eyes well trained in steamy bathhouses—all of which he sketches in these electric pages. This book parses queer spaces, the queer self, with a heart as intelligent and thoughtful as its author. As he proves in his unapologetic memoir, Gomez is a force to be reckoned with."

> —Matt Ortile, author of *The Groom Will Keep His Name*

"Edgar Gomez has written a memoir that stands out among so many others, with a narrative voice that's singularly hilarious and observant and unforgettable, so perfectly nuanced with memory and humor in limning the landscapes of love in Florida and Nicaragua. At the center is his mother, a bright vivid burst of fear and tenderness and absolute deep-hearted love. *High-Risk Homosexual* presents a brand new voice of impeccable clarity and vision."

> —Susan Straight, American Book Award finalist and author of *In The Country of Women*

"There's a rhythm to vulnerable, honest writing, and Edgar Gomez doesn't miss a beat in *High-Risk Homosexual*. His characters—his mother, his friends, his lovers—are his dance partners whom he lovingly dips and twirls across the page, their beauty on full display even as he bares their humanity and his own to the audience. This memoir is a master class in humor with warmth, not ridicule, and truth with tenderness, not overexposure. Pick this book up for the laughs, but have your tissue ready for a few tears too."

—Minda Honey, author of *An Anthology of Assholes*

"High-Risk Homosexual is a vivacious, compelling, and intimate portrait about queer coming-of-age and finding oneself. Gomez's writing has this special way of inviting us in, like an old friend, catching us up to the pains, doldrums, and pleasures of living, reminding us at every turn of the exquisite messiness that is life. This memoir is a sheer delight, and one not to be missed."

—Marcos Gonsalez, author of *Pedro's Theory:*
Reimagining the Promised Land

"Edgar Gomez is the chaotic queer hero we both need and deserve—with humor and charm, he tenderly leads us into night clubs, bathhouses, the back seat of cars with anonymous men, asking us to examine our current place in the world amongst the lonely and brokenhearted, the ones who dare live our truest lives. For anyone whose coming out and coming-of-age is messy in all the ways, let *High-Risk Homosexual* be a road map."

—Christopher Gonzalez, author of
I'm Not Hungry but I Could Eat

"High-Risk Homosexual is an absolute marvel in voice, style, and its raucous, tender, heartbreaking, compassionate, and ultimately triumphant examination of gay spaces, the politics of gender, violence against GLBTQ folks, and, of course, the human heart. Edgar Gomez is an unforgettable writer with enviously fantastic storytelling skills. You'll laugh, you'll cry, you'll rage, you'll buy this book for all of your friends."   —Emily Rapp Black, author of *Sanctuary* and
Frida Kahlo and My Left Leg

High-Risk
Homosexual

High-Risk
Homosexual

A Memoir

EDGAR GOMEZ

Soft Skull
New York

This is a work of nonfiction. However, some names and identifying
details of individuals have been changed to protect their privacy,
correspondence has been shortened for clarity, and dialogue has
been reconstructed from memory.

First Soft Skull edition: 2022

Library of Congress Cataloging-in-Publication Data
Names: Gomez, Edgar (Writer), author.
Title: High-risk homosexual : a memoir / Edgar Gomez.
Description: New York, NY : Soft Skull Press, [2022]
Identifiers: LCCN 2020057113 | ISBN 9781593767051 (paperback) |
ISBN 9781593767068 (ebook)
Subjects: LCSH: Gomez, Edgar (Writer) | Hispanic American
gays—United States—Biography. | Gay men—United States—
Biography. | Coming out (Sexual orientation)—United States.
Classification: LCC HQ75.8.G72 A3 2022 | DDC 306.76/62092
[B]—dc23
LC record available at https://lccn.loc.gov/2020057113

Cover design & Soft Skull art direction by www.houseofthought.io
Book design by Wah-Ming Chang

Published by Soft Skull Press
New York, NY
www.softskull.com

Printed in the United States of America
5 7 9 10 8 6

For my mother, La Terrible, and my brother, Maracas

You and your causes! Look, that child is Latin.
You don't wanna be gettin' mixed up in all that Latin mess.
She might turn out to be a Sandinista or something.

NOXEEMA JACKSON
To Wong Foo, Thanks for Everything! Julie Newmar

Two Disclaimers

First, throughout this book, I use the words *Latino/a* and *Latinx*. The latter, pronounced latin-ex, is a more inclusive term meant to make room for transgender and gender non-conforming people in the community. Neither of these words are perfect, and the idea of a Latinx community in general is itself overly broad and historically anti-Black and anti-Indigenous. Until there's a better way to describe our complicated identities, I use *Latino/a/x* with the understanding that I mean anyone who identifies as such, and that includes Black and Indigenous people.

Second, while this is a work of nonfiction, the names and identifying features of some individuals have been changed to protect privacy, and conversations were reconstructed to the best of my ability. Please don't sue me.

Contents

High-Risk
Homosexual

Introduction

What Is a Boy?

Moments after I was born at the Mount Sinai Medical Center of Greater Miami, my parents were handed a document, which I stumbled upon years later, curled and yellow at the edges, inside of a shoebox in a corner of my closet. It told them everything they needed to know about me, like a pamphlet you might find in the packaging of a new blender. My birthday: March 5, 1992. Birth time: 1:44 a.m. Weight: 8 lbs., 5 oz. There's even an imprint of my newborn feet, so small I could hold them both in the palm of one hand. Of course I'm fascinated by them, because they're mine, but I don't know why anyone else would be interested enough to press my soles to ink and have them preserved forever. I'm not entirely sure what medical or governmental purpose my little feet serve. I wasn't asked for a copy of them when I applied for a driver's permit, or a passport, or when I signed up for the drug that would lead me to being diagnosed a high-risk homosexual. This document is not a birth certificate. It's something else, I think. An instruction manual.

Taking up almost half the page, a poetic sketch of what my parents should expect of their newborn is nested under the heading What Is a Boy?

Between the innocence of babyhood and the dignity of manhood we find a delightful creature called a boy. Boys come in assorted sizes, weights and colors, but all boys have the same creed: to enjoy every second of every minute of every hour of every day and to protest with noise (their only weapon) when their last minute is finished and the adult males pack them off to go to bed at night.

Boys are found everywhere—on top of, underneath, inside of, climbing on, swinging from, running around, or jumping to. Mothers love them, little girls hate them, older sisters and brothers tolerate them, adults ignore them, and Heaven protects them.

A boy is a magical creature—you can lock him out of your living room, but you can't lock him out of your heart. You can get him out of your study, but you can't get him out of your mind. Might as well give up—he is your captor, your jailor, your boss, and your master—a freckled-face, pint-sized, cat-chasing, bundle of noise.

Yes, he is a nerve-wracking nuisance, just a noisy bundle of mischief. But when your dreams tumble down and the world is a mess—when it seems you are pretty much a fool—he can make it all perfect when he climbs on your knee and whispers, "I love you best of all!"

When I first discovered the document, after snort-laughing for ten minutes, I wondered what my parents, who do not read English, would have thought had they been given a translated copy. Would they have been worried, like I was, at the oddly threatening tone in "he is your captor, your jailor, your boss"? Would they have been confused, asking themselves whether the "freckled-face" child the anonymous author describes was supposed to be me? Worse, would they have agreed that this, in fact, is what a boy is?

After all, so many of the boys—and the "adult males"— in my life might have seen themselves reflected in these lines. The words could easily refer to any of my tíos, or my older brother, or my father, who my mother left while I was still in elementary school. I don't think it's a mistake that no author is attributed, because the passage belongs to all of us. Despite my initial instinct to laugh the document off, I see myself in it too.

A boy is not something you're born as, but rather an identity you inherit—this piece of paper, if nothing else, is proof of that. Spanish speakers call that inheritance *machismo*, defined as a strong or aggressive masculine pride, though male chauvinism is hardly a Latin American invention. Beyond the cliché that men must marry, spawn children, and head their households, machismo extends to having a fiercely unapologetic outlook. Perhaps this is in response to European colonization, a refusal to bow down as a reclamation of power. Or maybe it's the result of the Catholic Church's long history of idolizing men. Either way, no apologies are given in real life, nor in this document, for the boy who is a "nerve-wracking nuisance," a "noisy bundle of mischief." It's not asked why "little girls hate them" or for what reason someone would lock them out of their study. As for the rooms that I locked myself in as a child, and those I was locked into, no apologies were ever given or expected. Apologies lead to emotions, and emotions are for delicate women, for the weak and the conquered. Overall it's a pretty sweet deal. Dudes can drink, fuck, and fight all we want *and* be magical creatures, protected by Heaven. In return it is only asked that our drink of choice be beer, that it's bodies that were born with vaginas we fuck, and that who we fight is anyone who wants to do otherwise. What kind of man would complain?

I've always found the definition of *machismo* to be ironic, considering that *pride* is a word almost unanimously associated with queer people, the enemy of machistas. In particular, effeminate queer men represent a simultaneous rejection and embrace of masculinity. We love men yet despise much of what being a so-called man entails. Even then, the lines separating us are not rigid. We can be just as sexist and arrogant as our heterosexual brothers. And of course, effeminate queer men can uphold machismo by prizing masculinity in our lovers, calling it a "preference" without interrogating why it is that we like who we like or doing anything to change that. While writing *High-Risk Homosexual*, I was time and again reminded of this catch-22: in a world desperate to erase us, queer Latinx men must find ways to hold on to pride for survival, but excessive male pride is often what we are battling, both in ourselves and in others. We threaten what we crave. This was true at my tío's cockfighting ring in Nicaragua, where the book opens, and in the gay bars, bathhouses, and bedrooms seen throughout its pages.

Like greed, fear, love, or any other aspect of humanity, machismo was never outright taught to me. I learned it, as did the older generations of men in my family, by living in communities where male expressions of affection were rare, where displays of sexual virility were praised, where women were expected to be silent and sacrifice their time, energy, pleasure, and sanity. If it weren't for my queerness, which made many of the benefits awarded to men who uphold machismo unappealing, I would have likely accepted them without question. The only way out, as the other cliché goes, is through, and the majority of us are left to do this blindly.

I am not under any delusion that my story presents a better instruction manual for boyhood than the one given to my parents. On some warped level, I'm grateful an instruction manual was given to them at all, even if it ultimately amounts to "Boys are from Hell. Enjoy." As I came of age, I longed for a guide to teach me how to navigate being a queer Latinx man. Lacking one, I pieced together my own rules based on the scarce examples I found around me of people attempting to find a new path: a bloody boy on the news, a group of transgender women on a street corner, a drag queen who introduced me to the possibility that we can decide who we are for ourselves. They were not enough, but I'm buoyed by the fact that queer people before me had even less, and the ones following in my own baby footsteps will have one more.

Malcriado

Mom peeled off one of her press-on nails and dropped it into her purse, the bag rattling between us, belly full of acrylics, as our cab crawled down the road. Outside, traffic to the airport was bumper-to-bumper, a mishmash of imports from all over the world: American school buses packed tight with families going to the market, Yamaha motorbikes on their last legs. Further out in the horizon, I could see dark towers of smoke rising up and melting into the ocean-blue sky. Trash burning. Cheaper, in Nicaragua, than sending it to landfills. I took a deep breath, savoring the faint, sweet scent of charred plastic and barbecue slipping into the car through the air conditioner. That smell always made me feel safe, the way the breeze carried it for miles and miles, how it shrouded the country like a thick, warm blanket. But it didn't work this time.

Now all I could think was that Mom would be on a plane headed back home to Orlando soon, flying through that stupid smoke, and that stupid sky, while I stayed behind without her for some stupid reason I didn't understand. I crossed my arms and huffed.

Of course I'd be fine, she was in the middle of telling the driver, loud enough for me to get that this speech wasn't for him. When my tíos, her brothers, barely had hair on their chests, the Sandinista army sent them to Cuba to learn to dismantle bombs. *They* didn't have their parents with them and *they* were okay. I'd heard this story a million times, and though the details often changed—sometimes just one of them went; sometimes they were torn out of my abuelita's arms—the point remained the same: boys in our family were tough. Mom peeled off another nail, half her fingers naked now, and leaned over the driver's seat.

"Besides," she said, voice swelling with pride. "My baby's practically a man already."

I was thirteen.

I rooted inside her purse and smuggled an acrylic back out, pressing it over one of my own badly chewed cuticles and admiring the way my ugly fingers transformed into a glamorous novela star's. Soraya Montenegro, draped in a silk kaftan. Catalina Creel, adjusting her eyepatch at her vanity table. For a second, imagining I was someone else, someone rich and beautiful and untouchable, helped me forget she was leaving me. I dove back in for more.

"Yeah, he'll be fine," the driver supposed. "What they did to kids back then . . ." He chuckled to himself. "Those crazy hijueputas."

Once I had a whole set on, I tapped Mom on the shoulder and held my new French manicure up to the window, gameshow-style. This part of Nicaragua, far from the coffee farms and volcanoes tourists flocked here for, looked just like Orlando, only with Spanish subtitles. A billboard down the road advertised McDonald's all-new menú de desayuno. On the sidewalk beside us, a pack of scrawny dogs nosed through a pile of garbage by a red ALTO sign.

The cab rolled to a stop.

Mom narrowed her eyes at my fingers, parting her lips to say something and then sealing them again. I knew that look. It was the same one she'd given me the day she walked into my bedroom and found me doing the choreography to Britney Spears's ". . . Baby One More Time" music video, my older brother Hector pointing a camcorder my way. Like she was working through a math problem. Dividing me in half. Solving for x. "It's for my demo reel. I'm sending it out to agents," I explained to her, and though I swear there was a touch of amusement in her eyes, that she'd wanted to smile like she did when I was younger and played with her dresses, she kept on staring, as if that only made the problem more difficult.

The cab took off again. In the rearview mirror, I spotted the driver watching us. So did Mom. She blushed and pulled my hands down into her lap.

"These aren't toys," she said, snatching the nails off my fingers.

"Yeah, I know. I was just messing around."

"Well, it's not funny. And your tíos won't think so either."

"I know," I said again. I did.

I knew this trip was important, so much so that she had to dump me in Nica with them for the next two weeks. I knew Hector couldn't come, because his grades weren't good. I knew she couldn't take any more days off work, because we couldn't afford it. I know I know I know.

"Don't be a malcriado," she said. "And put those sad eyes away. I don't want to find out from your tíos you acted like some pobrecito the whole time you were here. When I was your age, what I would have given . . ." She dug an elastic band out of her purse and tied her mane of copper-tinted hair into a ponytail. A couple hours after her flight, she was scheduled to clock in to her job at the Orlando airport Starbucks. If she finished getting ready now, she could sleep the whole four-hour ride. "You don't realize how lucky you are. How expensive plane tickets are." She sighed and continued under her breath: "¡Dios mío, dame paciencia con este niño!"

I turned around and peeked through the rear window to see if my uncles were still following us in their pickup truck. Maybe I was lucky, like she said. Maybe they got into a horrible car accident. She'd have to delay her flight home or, better, take me with her.

But no, there they were, Tío Alvaro hunched over behind the wheel and Tío César standing on the cargo bed guarding Mom's suitcases. As our cab weaved through a gap in traffic, Tío Alvaro pounded on the horn for the driver to slow down.

Tío César pumped his fist in the air to the honks as if he were at a rock concert, his gray hair flapping around him in the wind. The driver started honking in return, all three men laughing while people on the street ogled the strange parade. I slunk down in my seat.

Two weeks. I'd never been alone with them that long. Even on other trips when Mom needed to get back to work, Hector had always been with me. It didn't make sense for him not to be here. His grades couldn't have been *that* bad. And he would have loved what my tíos had planned. Tío Alvaro said we were going to the gallera, his cockfighting ring, this weekend, and Tío César told me he was sneaking me into a bar for some "boy time" the next. If Hector had come, I could have let him take my place and stayed home watching cable. I didn't want to go to the gallera or a bar. I wanted to be left alone. I wanted my mom.

I buried my face in her armpit, wishing I could tell her why she couldn't leave me with my tíos, the secret ticking inside my chest, growing louder as the time closed between when I had her by my side and when I wouldn't. In less than an hour we would arrive at the airport and she'd be gone. Then there wouldn't be anyone left—not her, not Hector—to hide behind. It would just be me and them, two men who spent their childhoods dismantling bombs. Two boys who survived a war, grew up, and were once again being handed a disaster to prevent.

At least that's what I suspect the truth is now, after telling myself this story a million times.

•

Tío Alvaro and I made it to the gallera around midnight, late, though he wasn't worried. The best cockfights were saved until the owner showed up.

By day, Tío worked as an engineer, leaving home before sunrise with a greasy comb-over and a briefcase crammed with blueprints for expensive government projects: highways, bridges. With a good, steady paycheck like that, he was the one everyone in the family called when they needed help making rent. I imagine it had to have been a lot of pressure, carrying us. I also imagine that's the reason he built the gallera as far as he could from the freshly paved roads he hired men like Tío César to lay down, at the end of a skinny dirt street at the edge of Managua.

"Al fin, loco," the security guard on duty told Tío and me as we approached. He swung the rusty gate door open and stepped aside to let us through. "We were wondering when you were going to show! It's getting crowded in there."

That put a smile on Tío Alvaro's fat, toadish face. "Good!" He rubbed his hands together. "I need the money. You see I have a son now."

The guard smirked and patted me on the head. "That so? This your dad?" he asked.

I wriggled out from beneath his palm. My preferred greeting was a double kiss on the cheeks, just like Mom, though later I found out that was a trick of hers to make sure

I wasn't stealing her foundation. We wore the same shade: Maybelline, Rich Tan.

"No," I answered flatly. My biological father was in Puerto Rico. Or New Jersey. I think.

Tío forced a laugh and steered me to the dusty wooden stands before I could embarrass him further.

The guard was right. The gallera was packed shoulder to shoulder. Two seats were cleared for us in the front row at the same time that a pair of roosters were flung into the cramped clay arena, lit up from all around like a boxing ring. A clock suspended from a chain in the center of the cockpit counted down from ten minutes. The men in the audience reached for the loose bills in their pockets, elbowing each other to get a better look. None of it—the crowd, the money, the timer—meant anything to the roosters. Uninterested in the spotlight, they pecked at the steel blades the size of nail clippings attached to their feet, utterly baffled by each other.

Prepared for this, the referee dragged two hens out of tin-wire cages just outside of the ring. He passed them on to a pair of trained handlers, who in turn carried them toward the roosters. As the handlers drew nearer with the girls, the boys looked up from their feet, eyes widening in delight. Hens weren't allowed near them until fight nights. The boys hopped toward the girls they'd been starved of, heads cocked to the side, wings fanning out for a big hug.

Hey, ladies! they said. *How y'all doing?*

The hens blinked in response. They were paralyzed. Their

wings clipped. Their feet bound with zip ties. In their pow-
erlessness, they didn't even bother to cry out.

I was learning to keep quiet too. I was small for my age.
My relatives were beginning to talk. They were curious about
my walk, my lisp, my breeding.

Most nights I could hear Mom fighting with my stepdad through the thin walls of our house in Orlando, never
naming what they argued about directly, in their avoidance
making the outline of the bad thing more apparent, like a
bleeped-out word in a rap song.

"Put him in sports! Send him outside!" he'd scream. "Or
do you want him to end up a—"

"A what?" Mom would shriek back. "I know what I'm
doing! He's fine! You don't know what it's like for him without his—"

"So you're going to let him run around like some—"

"He's not. If he were . . . I'll deal with it!"

Hector would turn up the volume on our radio, while I
lay in bed reading Choose Your Own Adventure books front
to back, skipping the instructions so I would know every
possible path I could take and pick the best one. Hours later
Mom would burst into our room puffy-eyed.

"Can I sleep with you?" she'd ask, crawling into my bed.
"My baby. So beautiful, so handsome. You got your mamí's
looks. It's going to be okay. I love you. I love you so much.
Don't listen to that man. Talk to me. You hungry? You want
me to fix you something?"

I never answered her, because to speak would have been

to acknowledge that I could hear, which would have meant that I'd heard *them*. If that were true then I couldn't tell myself they didn't know my secret. Everything would be okay as long as I kept quiet.

That was the best path.

The handlers swung the tied-up hens in circles around each rooster, slowly at first to get their attention, then faster and faster, until the roosters were trapped in flesh hurricanes.

"¡Dale!" the handlers shouted. Come on!

Disoriented, the boys tried to claw their way out, thrusting their blades into the girls' necks. The girls took the hits in silence, their faces distant, cold.

"¡Dale, gallito! ¡Dale, hijuesumadre!" the handlers kept hollering, pissing the boys off. Once they were ready to fight, the handlers lifted the girls out of reach.

Suddenly alone again, the boys kicked at the dirt. They beat their heads into the arena walls. They looked for someone to blame for scaring away the chicks, found a pair of beady black eyes staring back at them in the ring. *You*, those dark eyes said. *This is your fault.*

Their jobs complete, the hens were passed on to a third handler, who wiped the blood from their faces and wings with a rag and turned them over in his hands. Satisfied they were in decent condition, he pressed his lips to each of their beaks and sucked out the blood lodged in their throats. Spat it into the dirt. Dove in, sucked out more, spat, more, spat, until finally his saliva ran clear. The kisses lasted no more than a few seconds, just long enough to save the girls' lives. When he was done, he wiped the blood from his mouth and shut them back in their cages.

Tío César gave me until the end of his drink to go talk to her. We were in a bar wedged between a dentist's office and a karate studio in a shopping plaza a fifteen-minute drive from his house, our tabletop decorated with laminated pictures of celebrities cut out from magazines. Beyoncé on a red carpet. Shakira grinning over her shoulder. Tío held his glass to his nose, squinted at the few sips of dark liquor left, then set it down over a woman whose face I didn't know. The fabric of his novelty T-shirt was stretched taut over his beer belly. An arrow on his chest pointed up to his red-splotched cheeks—"The Hero"—another down at his bulge—"The Legend."

Tonight better not be a waste. He wasn't rich like Tío Alvaro. Unemployed except for the occasional construction gig, he probably had to scrounge for the money to bribe the doorman to let me in. For what? So I could bite my nails all night?

"Get over there," Tío César said, pointing his bottom lip at a figure at the end of the bar. "Ask her to dance. I mean, c'mon, look at those *legs!*"

I followed his lips to those legs, brown with mosquito bites in various stages of healing peppered across them. She wasn't some random girl. No, I vaguely recognized her from other trips to Nica when I was younger, on her knees, scrubbing the floor. She was Tío Alvaro's former housekeeper.

What was she doing here? She wore a pretty lilac dress with delicate spaghetti straps, something that belonged swishing around on a homecoming dance floor, not in some bar a few feet away from where people got their cavities filled. I couldn't remember her name, or when I'd last seen her. She seemed much older at the time but must have only been around seventeen: a girl-woman. Me: a girly-boy.

"You can't tell me you don't want a piece of that!" Tío said. His thinning gray hair was plastered with sweat across his forehead. The strands looked like scars from old scratches.

"Why did she get fired?" I asked.

He downed the last of his rum and coke, then, not wasting a minute, ordered three more. Three. He waved a glass in the air. The girl-woman floated over. She introduced herself by taking the drink from his hands and smiling like she didn't know me.

Tío stole a seat from the table next to ours. The girl-woman sat down and swayed to the music, shook her big curly hair around. In the disco lighting, her face was streaked neon red. She had the sultry, sleepy eyes of a Bratz doll.

"You used to work for my tío, right?" I asked.

She shrugged and took a long sip from her drink. "Come on, let's dance!"

"I don't really know how," I said, shuddering at the thought of having to hold her. Press her to me. Tío watching, expecting us to do something.

"Really?" She pouted and touched my knee with her hand.

"You go if you want," I said, pulling my leg in.

Her eyes shifted from Tío to me to him again, a mixture of angry and embarrassed and confused. Who did I think I was, some kid holding his drink with a napkin, wearing a baseball cap to look older, turning *her* down? Before I could make up a lie about being too tired, Tío whispered something into her ear that made her giggle and push his chest. One of her dress straps slipped over her shoulder, dangling just below the pale vaccine scar in her arm. She left it there.

I chugged the rest of my rum and coke.

The next thing I knew, our table was full of empty bottles. Then Tío César was gone. It was just me and her, ordering another round of shots. Me and her, two tangled bodies on the cramped dance floor. How we got there and where Tío had gone I couldn't say; neither of us cared. It happened in a blink, in the change of a song, and suddenly we were best friends and it was very important that I know how to move. I placed my hands on her waist and maneuvered us around in sloppy circles. Her claws dug into my back when I dipped her. Our faces flashed blue and purple and green. She tried not to laugh at my attempt to lead. I loved her for that. When she finally couldn't hold it back and dropped to the ground in hysterics, I loved her more. Maybe it was the alcohol, or that I still had hope that whatever was wrong with me would go away, but for a moment it seemed possible: I really could. Love her.

"You're awful!" she screamed from the floor. "Didn't anyone teach you *anything*?"

I picked her up and tried again. To Luis Enrique's "Yo No Se Mañana" and Frankie Ruiz's "Bailando." Till the sound of horns and maracas melted into the bartender yelling last call. Till Tío César finally appeared, shaking his car keys over our heads.

Minutes later Tío drummed his fingers on the steering wheel to the Spanish rock song on the radio. Between us, the girl-woman dozed, her head resting on my shoulder. The weight of it pushed my body against the passenger door. Beyond my window the streets swirled by.

"Hey," I whispered, pinching her thigh. She groaned and raked my chest in protest. "Wake up," I tried again. My head was spinning. From the drinks, from the gradual realization that we weren't dropping her off. "Come on," I said, but I could feel myself drifting away too.

The hens watched from their cages as the roosters aimed their steel blades at each other's throats.

Cockfighting roosters are regal, not at all like the scraggly chickens you might see on a farm. Once in the ring, they're given names based on the colors of their luxurious coats. Rojito, Red, my uncle's pick for the match, was more of a *merlot*, a shade I knew from going hair-dye shopping with Mom. His chest was *mahogany*. His tail feathers, spreading out behind him like a paper fan, *age-defying platinum*. And Chocolate wasn't really brown. He was *chestnut*. He was red. Red on his beak where Rojito licked him with his blade. Red on his wings. A pool of red sinking into the clay dirt by his feet.

"Oye, hombre, I hope you're hungry for chicken soup!" Tío Alvaro yelled at Chocolate's handler.

I turned my eyes from the fight. Focused on the men around me—skin glistening, arms waving money up high, mouths tearing into plates of carne asada, stretching the steak out with their teeth, the meat thinning, snapping. The air thick with the smell of beer and, because the bathroom was simply wherever you could find privacy, piss. On the side of the arena, leaning against the ring's wooden enclosure, an off-duty handler wiped his bare chest with a dirty rag. His pants sat just below his waist. I could see the band of his underwear, a line of hair trailing down his damp belly like a finger giving directions. I wanted to lick him, take my tongue and follow the . . .

Shit, I was staring. I shut my eyes. I couldn't look at the ring, where Chocolate was tipped over and draining out as Rojito hacked at him with his talons, couldn't trust myself not to look at *him*. In the dark, I sensed Tío Alvaro's gaze on me, appraising me like I was one of his animals.

The summer before, I learned from a man on TV that lizards can regenerate a lost appendage within sixty days. That afternoon, I climbed a tree with a butter knife and pinned one down by its tail. For a second after I brought the knife down, the lizard stayed still, as if it didn't know yet what I'd done, or worse: it did know, and it was afraid there was more to come. Then, in a flash, it was gone, leaving its bloody limb writhing behind it.

It wasn't much, but it was everything, because it was when the idea first hatched in my mind: you can lose a part of yourself to save the rest.

I heard the referee count down from fifteen, to ten, to nine, and opened my eyes so Tío Alvaro wouldn't think I was too sissy to watch. Chocolate thrashed on the ground. Just give up, I tried to tell him with my thoughts, waving my hands in the air like all the men around me. Save yourself, idiot. If he played dead, the referee would call the match. If he gave up, he could live.

The girl-woman and I lay on a twin-sized bed in a corner of a bedroom in Tío César's house. The lights flicked off, the door slammed shut, the gears in the knob clicked. Tío's footsteps faded down the hallway. We were locked in.

I could smell her fruity perfume next to me. Sour candy. Vodka. My BO. Our sweaty bar clothes clung to our skin. I didn't know what to do, if she was waiting for me to start. I'd seen porn before, watched silhouettes twisting together on the grainy channels our cable box didn't quite get. Were we supposed to undress, or kiss? I'd never kissed anyone. What if I didn't do it right? Would she know me from my lips? What I was? Would she be able to taste me on me?

"Are you okay?" I asked her.

She hesitated a moment, then answered, quietly, "Yes."

"Okay."

One of my shoulders was pressed against a wall, the other half an inch from her. I hadn't gotten her name, and at this point it seemed rude to ask. I only knew her for what she wasn't. She was the former housekeeper, and she'd been fired for some reason no one wanted to tell. To get out, I would have to climb over her, confess to Tío that I couldn't do it. I was trapped. I brought my arms into myself.

Outside, through an open window, the sound of a whistle pierced through the night. The neighborhood watchman, paid fifteen bucks a month to roam the streets making noise so burglars would know not to come here. I wondered if he did a good job scaring thieves, why my uncle was so insistent on me having sex with this stranger, why he had to lock the door. Didn't he trust that I wanted this?

My chest tightened. No. No no no no.

Mom leaving. Hector not being here. The girl-woman.

It hit me: This wasn't just about me losing my virginity, which is what I'd guessed back at the bar. He knew. They knew. I was meant to lose something else entirely.

Would they believe me? If I told them how sorry I was. That I didn't mean to be like this. If I promised to be good, would they let me go back to my room in Orlando, where I could make myself disappear inside one of my books? I'd be better. I'd try harder. I'd play sports and go to church and talk to more girls at school and . . . and . . . nothing. Nothing would be enough, because I hurt my mom. All she ever did was love me and I'd made her sad, pushed her far away. I deserved that. I deserved to be alone. In my peripheral vision, the girl-woman's body shifted slightly.

Isn't he too young? she must have been asking herself. Maybe she thought it was a joke when Tío asked her to come home with us, with me, when he pulled us into the room and patted the sheets on the bed. Or maybe she didn't. She did get in, after all. Maybe she knew exactly what the job was, knew it at the bar and knew it here, even as my heart ticked desperately beside her. But this wasn't what she signed up for.

Before, she might have been able to tell herself I wanted to. Obviously, she had to have realized by now that I didn't. That made two of us. How to get out of here? She would have to knock on the door, ask Tío to let us go. Was there enough cash in her purse for a cab ride home? And what, if she was thinking about this at all, would Tío do to me if he found out nothing happened? No, she couldn't change her mind. She was trapped.

I counted. One, two, three. Breathe. One, two, three. Don't explode.

"Are you okay?" she asked.

I hesitated a moment, then answered, quietly, "Yes."

"Okay."

Lying there in the dark, baffled by each other, without moving or speaking, we agreed, *I won't tell if you won't.* There was a timer on us. There was a man waiting.

How long does it take for a boy to become a man?

That's how long we waited.

The gallera grew manic as the night dragged along. The air full with a wild, frenzied energy. The winners electrified by their new money. The losers furious to make it back. One of the handlers pounded on his chest, his shirt tucked into his back pocket to use to wipe the blood off his birds between rounds. Chocolate lay in a corner of the ring with a towel draped over him. His feet poked out, blades still attached. Chicken soup.

Tío Alvaro, who, as the owner, could never lose even if he lost, wrapped his arm around me, handed me a twenty-dollar bill, and ordered me to place his next bet. His phone buzzed lightly over the din of the crowd. My aunt. When are you coming home? When he was done, Jesus, he intoned into the receiver, cool as ever, and snapped his phone shut. Two more roosters were plucked from their cages and flung into the ring.

Even now, years later, I don't know how intricately this trip was orchestrated, whether Mom told my tíos to step in, or if they decided on their own to help their sister who always had a weak stomach for things like this. What would always nag me, though, beyond anyone else's complicity, is my own. As much as my family wanted me to be a man, I wanted it more. I knew how boys who didn't teach themselves how to fight ended up. I remembered watching one of them on the news with Mom. His eyes veiled behind a black censor box, arms sliced up. Pictures of a machete and rainbow dog tags flashing on-screen. I knew enough to fill in the pieces of the story the reporter missed, to not question

Mom when she turned the TV off and said, "Pandilleros," as if things like that only happened to people in gangs.

Inside the ring a handler approached the clock to reset it by hand. The new chickens weaved between his legs. Black. Brown. Tío shot me The Look. Adding up how long I hesitated, subtracting the number of times I'd ever mentioned a girl.

"Twenty on Negrito!" I blurted out. But the match hadn't even begun.

"Twenty!" I tried again. No one took the bet.

"Ten?" Nothing.

Tío smiled, pulled me closer, and held me in the crook of his arm. "Relax," he whispered into my ear. "Wait for the next one." I exhaled and repeated the same thing to myself. No need to panic yet. Tío César said next week he was taking me to a dance club. Maybe there I'd change.

In the meantime, two roosters skirted around the arena, wondering how they got there and who these men watching were.

A key rattled inside the doorknob. The lock clicked. The girl-woman and I turned to each other. *Hurry.* I clawed my jeans open. She pulled her dress down and tousled my hair. A dagger of light from the hallway cut through the room. Tío César stood in the doorframe surveying the scene through glossy pink eyes. He nodded in approval.

We called her a cab. One second it was there and she

was crawling inside; then it was gone, disappearing with her name into the night. I followed Tío back into the house. Without another word he sank into the living room couch and turned on the TV. A small mercy. The glow of the screen eclipsed any need to discuss what went down between us.

I stumbled toward the room where the girl-woman and I had been trapped, to the bathroom, and washed the sweat off my face over the sink. Woozy from the drinks I had at the bar and stuck somewhere between fight and flight, I stared into the mirror so long my reflection went vague. Two dark smudges where my eyebrows were, my lips a red blob. I blinked and came into focus. I blinked again, but the trick stopped working. Everything was as clear as it was going to get. This was next time. I had a chance and I didn't take it.

There was no way I could return to that bed, not right now. I crept out into the living room and found Tío César with his chin tucked into his chest, his mouth chewing on something in his sleep, then tiptoed up the stairs, careful not to wake him up.

When I reached the second floor, I grabbed a bottle of Flor de Caña from the minibar and poured myself a tall, warm glass of rum, filling it to the brim. As I set it back on the bar counter, I noticed that someone, probably one of Tío César's buddies, had forgotten a joint and some matchsticks. I snatched them too and walked out onto the balcony, softly closing the door behind me.

A few feet away, a streetlamp beamed, the bulb close enough to reach out and touch. Mosquitos swam in the golden air around it. I fumbled lighting the joint. Half of it was scorched by the time I had a smooth, even burn going. The smoke tingled on my lips, tasting deceptively sweet as it crawled along my tongue before suddenly scratching the back of my throat. I hacked into my arm, my lungs rapidly expanding and shriveling up again. The edges of my vision fizzled as tears filled my eyes. I'd never been high. It was nice, like being erased.

Tío's house was planted at the intersection of two busy commercial roads. All around me the indifferent sounds of the neighborhood turned up in my ears. Random honks from cars driving by, giggling coming upstairs from the wide wraparound porch anyone on the block was welcome to use. Drunks, I assumed, winding down after a long night.

I held the glass of rum to my lips and said it, just to see what would happen: "Gay." I took a sip and swallowed. The word slipped under the burning feeling sinking into my chest.

My life didn't blow up, but I didn't feel any relief either. I felt like . . . like . . .

Like I understood why novela villains were always laughing and sobbing and throwing chairs. Had everyone left me alone I would have kept believing I was just going through a phase, that one day soon I would start liking who I was supposed to. Instead, by forcing me to confront myself, now I knew exactly who I was. It'd almost be funny if it weren't so terrifying, if I didn't want to smash my glass on the street and scream.

The giggles on the porch grew louder, mocking my big dramatic moment. I peered over the railing and squinted through the dark. There were four of them down there. One wore a leopard-print top and miniskirt. Another a silk black dress with a butterfly brooch. Now I understand they were trans women, but back then, when I only knew there were people like me and people like everyone else, I thought they were just girly-boys.

I was beginning to doubt they were real when the one in the miniskirt spotted me.

"¡Oye, lindo!" she called up.

Her friends joined in.

"You live in that nice house?"

"All by yourself?"

"You got a girlfriend, cutie?" the redhead of the group asked. "You want one?"

"No!" I shouted, surprising myself. I was talking to her. We were talking. A line of smoke from the cigarette tucked in her mouth trailed up and merged with the smoke from my joint. She raised a razor-thin eyebrow at the tone in my voice.

"I mean, nah," I tried again. "I already have one."

"Yeah, yeah." She grabbed her ass and winked. "Well, if you change your mind."

It was a slow night. High up on the balcony, I watched as the girls adjusted their wigs and reapplied lip gloss, dragging the wands across their lips without bothering to remove their cigarettes. When a rare car cruised by, they quickly spread out in the middle of the street, lined up side by side, and modeled their outfits. Every now and then drivers would hit the breaks to get a better look. Almost always they changed their minds when they realized the same thing I had, then sped away in a flurry of horns. The girls chased after them, hurling their cigarettes, lit ends flying through the air like emergency flares.

"¡Cochón! You don't like women!" they yelled, marching back to the porch and sparking new ones. After a few seconds the laughter started up again.

I knew I should go inside. If the watchman saw me remotely near them, he'd tell Tío César, and he'd tell Mom. This was exactly what she was scared of, that I would end up like *these* people. Plopped down on the corner of some street, making myself known. It was sex work. It was dangerous. And it likely wasn't a choice. But they made it seem so fun.

"You got anything for us, baby?" one of them eventually asked me, growing more daring as the watchman's whistle faded further away.

I stepped aside to a corner of the balcony where the streetlight was dimmest, just in case.

"What are you smoking?" her friend chimed in. "You don't share?"

By now, the joint was barely long enough to hold between my fingers. I'd wasted most of it in my pathetic attempt to get it started.

"There's not a lot!" I answered, both embarrassed and delighted I had anything to offer at all.

"Dale pues," she cooed back. "We don't mind."

I tossed the stump into the air, keeping my eye on it as it fluttered down and landed on the porch. The girls gathered round and passed it among themselves.

I was so generous, they said, such a good boy, so handsome.

They reminded me of Mom at her best, those nights that put her on the defensive against my stepdad. Of course I wasn't spoiled. I wasn't a malcriado. I was just like her. Her face. Her shade. Her baby. That was the problem.

I wanted to stay up on the balcony talking to them. There were so many things I was dying to ask. Who were they? Did their families hate them? Was Mom going to hate me? Were they happy? But Tío was one floor away, the watchman bound to return soon. Of all the paths I could take, being seen with them was the riskiest. The smartest thing to do would be to go back to my room, fall asleep, wake up the next day, and act like we'd never met.

In one of the million other stories I've since told myself about that night, there was no one there to stop us. I wasn't nervous the watchman would hear or see me as the sun began to rise. The girls and I spoke and laughed for hours, tipsy, stoned, safe.

You know you're perfect, right? they said before turning to go.

And this time I didn't stay quiet. Didn't crawl into my mind and hide. I told them what I hoped was the truth, the thing my favorite person said to me after every fight, when she climbed into my bed and promised it would all be okay.

Thank you, I said. *I got it from my mom.*

Straight Acting

I was waiting for a love like in the movies—one of the romantic comedies I spent hours watching every night when Mom and my stepdad fell asleep, after their arguments about rent and putas and me dissolved into gentle snores, and I could finally pretend I lived alone in our little blue house in Orlando.

As soon as their bedroom door closed, I would move quickly, slipping out from beneath my covers and padding barefoot on the cold tile into the kitchen. From a cabinet above the stove I'd pull out one of the bags of Starbucks dark roast Mom stole from work, then brew myself an extra-strong batch. If I could see through the pot, it was too weak. If it was thick and black, I'd take it to the couch, burrito myself with a blanket, and pound back mug after mug, sweat spreading across my forehead as the caffeine flooded through my veins. I don't know where I learned how to do this, but it worked, so long as I pushed on. I drank until my throat was raw, until my fingertips went numb and my heartbeat crossed from panic into euphoria. One more sip and my vision fogged up from dehydration. Another and, at last, my life faded to black:

Tío's housekeeper and the trip to Nicaragua. Getting expelled from high school the very next year when a friend caught selling weed named me as an accomplice. What the superintendent told Mom shortly before sending me to my new school, Oak Ridge.

Just, he'd sighed, *watch him.*

When I was buzzed on coffee, the past disappeared, and all I could focus on was keeping my hands still enough to scroll through the DVR, which I'd filled entirely with rom-coms the second Hector went away to college in Miami. My favorites featured ethnically ambiguous women (Jennifer Lopez) who were victims of circumstance (poor) and overcame the odds through sheer force of will (were rescued by rich white dudes). *Maid in Manhattan. Monster-in-Law. Enough.*

No one needed to tell me Jennifer and I were the same person. I was half Puerto Rican. We were both tan. With similar last names: Gomez. Lopez. We could have easily traded places. *I* was the damsel in distress. It was only a matter of time before *my* rich white dude came for me.

On her way out to her opening shifts at the airport Starbucks, Mom occasionally stopped to watch a bit of the movie I'd chosen. I poured her a cup of coffee, and the two of us would sit there in silence while, on-screen, Jennifer got her heel caught in sewer grates, tripped on sidewalk cracks, men always waiting there to scoop her up. This late at night, or early in the morning for Mom, both of us were too tired to do more than watch. I wasn't her disappointing son. She wasn't my overwhelmed mother. We were girlfriends at the movies, losing ourselves for a few hours. Three thirty passed. She kissed me goodbye on the forehead. Four o'clock.

Time to get ready for school.

First I drew X's on my hands; that way I could blame my exhaustion on spending all night at a made-up bar. Then I put on the baggiest shirt I could find, cinched my pants around my waist using a shoelace, and accessorized with anywhere from two to five rosaries I paid for with money I made selling candy bars. Lastly, I tried really hard to go to the bathroom.

This step was the most important, more than my costume, because on campus I insisted to anyone who would listen that I never, ever pooped.

"I just sweat everything out," I'd say.

It was kind of my thing.

The trick I used to distract people from what was right in front of them.

No, I wasn't a fag. I was just weird. Or hetero-adjacent. Like Prince.

Drained from pulling another all-nighter, I sleepwalked through my morning classes, dozing in the back during math and science, dreaming about having a boyfriend. By noon the caffeine's narcotic effect would wear off, and I'd wake up both heartbroken and relieved to be alone, my secret still safe. Wandering through the hallways at Oak Ridge, my life faded up again in sharp, biting clarity.

I wasn't Jennifer Lopez. We were never trading places. No one was coming for me. Even if there was, how would he ever see me while I was in the closet?

When October came, I gave myself permission to sign up for the school musical, figuring I'd earned enough freak credits to finally do something gay. As an extra precaution, I doubled the number of rosaries I wore to the first day of rehearsal and sat far away from everyone else.

Mr. King, our drama teacher, had on the same wrinkled Hawaiian shirt he was wearing when I auditioned. Now, he roamed between the tables arranged around his classroom, stopping next to each member of the cast so he could introduce us with an icebreaker question.

"Edgar!" he announced when he reached me. He pushed up his gold-framed glasses and read my name from a notepad in his hand. "Or do you prefer Eddy?"

"Edgar," I said.

He brought the notepad down.

"How about you tell us an interesting fact about yourself?"

"Um." I shrugged, wishing this was over so the attention would be off me. "I guess I like movies."

"What kind?" he pressed on.

I opened my mouth to answer, then caught myself.

"Horror," I said. "I love . . . blood."

He smiled politely and moved on.

Twenty minutes later, as Mister stood at the head of the room setting up the VCR, Angel, one of the gospel choir kids, strolled in.

Pst pst, he whispered into Mister's ear—probably his excuse for not being on time.

From my seat I could see the soft outline of basketball shorts under Angel's tight jeans. He must have run out of clean underwear that morning. I crossed my legs, imagining that.

Pst pst, he kept whispering, and it almost looked like he was giving Mister stage directions: nod seriously, shake your head, nod again, now say—

"Oh, shoosh." Mister patted Angel's back. "You get one free pass. Go on. Time is of the essence, dear."

The chair next to me groaned as Angel pulled it out and slid into it. I pretended not to notice: his fade haircut, the two cubic zirconia studs pinched into his ears, every empty seat around me he could have taken. Mister stood in front of the room and asked, "Any of y'all already familiar with the musical *Working*?"

Angel averted his eyes. I peered over at the sad little rich girl sitting at the table next to ours. Sad Little Rich Girl was always stoned and depressed about something: what they did to Joan of Arc, horses' rights. I'd only been at Oak Ridge for a few months, but I knew her parents, who were, like, lawyers, flew her to New York all the time to watch Broadway shows to lift her spirits. She might have known *Working*, though maybe not at that exact moment. Right before rehearsal some kids at the bus stop had dared her to try to finish a joint in a single drag.

"Milkshake!" she'd screamed, wrapping her lips around the filter end and sucking until her American Eagle jeans were littered with ash.

Now she gaped at the blinking red light on the VCR as if it were lecturing her about global warming in Morse code. Of the handful of white girls on campus, I liked her most. She never asked for discounts on candy.

"Okay," Mister said. He coughed into his fist in that obviously fake way. "That's okay."

In the seventies, he told us, this famous journalist went around the country talking to people about where they worked and whether they liked their jobs. A lot of them said no, they were just doing what they had to do to pay their bills. Some at least had enough dignity to lie, like the valet attendant who swore he was famous in China. Or the waitress who insisted her job was an art form—balancing plates, she said, was a ballet! I pictured her rushing to the bathroom between orders and slicing her thighs with a spork to see if she could *feel something*.

When the journalist finished the interviews, he realized they all sounded pretty catchy when put to music, so he adapted the workers' stories into a Broadway show. Three

decades later, Mister decided we'd put it on. He handed us
scripts with our characters' lines highlighted.

I was Office Worker #3. I peeked over at Angel's. Office
Worker #1.

Mister flicked the lights off with his elbows and pressed
play on the VCR so we could see how it was done by
professionals.

As the room darkened, the air conditioner made a
phlegmy, congested noise. Angel folded his arms into a pillow and laid his head down. Cold air blew out of the vents
in the ceiling. Up close, I could see his prickly black arm
hairs silhouetted against the grainy television screen, where
a cleaning lady scrubbed the floors of an office building.

The only time her daughter would be on her knees, she
wailed, would be to pray.

I focused on the goosebumps rising along Angel's arms.
With everyone's eyes on the TV, the two of us were on a
private island. What if, the question slunk into my mind,
he . . . I don't know . . . *wasn't* straight? He sat next to you.
He sat next to *you*. That had to mean something.

I inched my arm close to his. All Angel needed to do was
feel my warmth, lift his head, whisper an interesting fact
about himself: I want to kiss you too.

I could already see us as an old married couple being pro-
filed for a magazine about the secret to our longevity, the
reporter desperate to know how we'd met.

"Well," Angel would say. "*I* was Office Worker #1." He'd
giggle and grab my hand.

"And *I* was Office Worker #3 . . ." I'd finish for him, winking in a way that would encapsulate everything missing in the dot dot dot. The desperate make-out session we had in the bathroom after that first rehearsal. His sister's illness, when I was really there for him. The wedding on a boat. Our magical rom-com life.

I waited for him to notice me, moving my arm nearer and nearer.

An hour and a half later, Mister flipped the lights back on. Angel was asleep.

Bianca, Mister's student-assistant, was watching me. I could feel her gaze on my back, following me through her thick cat-eye prescription lenses. There was something off about my energy, my look.

I dressed like a Christian rapper.

Had a drug record.

Loved blood.

These were all clear signs I was trouble. Added to her case, two weeks into rehearsals, she discovered I couldn't sing in falsetto.

We were onstage, assigning the roles for "If I Could've Been," the group number where the workers finally admit their lives aren't as merry as they'd let on in their interviews. At the part where we all look to the sky and squint, fantasizing about all the great things we could have done if life hadn't knocked us down, we were supposed to hit a soaring, hopeful high note. The lyrics did soar out of my mouth, but they quickly lost control and farted around the air like a deflating balloon.

Bianca shut the lid on the beat-up piano in front of her and crossed her arms at me. "Can I tell you what your problem is?" she asked straightaway.

I was tone-deaf?

"You're scared of sounding girly, just like all teenage boys." Her hand reached in and out of her book bag, where a box of Honey Nut Cheerios was nested among her flavored lip balms. She calmly munched away as she made her diagnosis. "That's why *I* only date *men*. Miss me with that machista mess."

Out of all the disguises I put on every morning, I never imagined anyone would peg me for a machista, a word I'd only heard spoken aloud on court-room shows like *Caso Cerrado*. Machistas were deadbeat husbands, broody, mean, the kind of dudes who called waitresses "baby." They were men like my stepdad. From the day Hector and I met him, when Mom dragged my brother and me from Miami to Orlando after divorcing our father, he refused to look or speak to either of us, lowering his eyes to the ground whenever we entered the same room as him at home.

At first we assumed he was shy and tried to win him over: Hector lingered beside him while he worked on junk cars in the front yard; I brought him iced tea. But nothing changed. After a while we decided he simply had no interest in being the father to two half-grown kids.

The little I knew about him I gathered from the ghostlike evidence of his presence he left around the house: beard clippings in the sink, a garbage bag full of crushed Tecate cans in the trash. Occasionally I heard him singing old Mexican rancheras in the kitchen when he must have thought I wasn't home. That was more disturbing than his silence. It was proof he was capable of affection; he just didn't have any for me.

For Bianca to lump us together was . . . perfect. She couldn't have had better timing.

Only a week before, a senior named Lee almost outed me.

We'd been in the costume closet while the rest of the cast was out on lunch break when he extended his hand to shake. I'd seen him on campus before—in the cafeteria, drawing rainbows in the white squares of his Vans checkerboard slip-ons; at the end of pointed fingers, basketball players laughing at him and his boyfriend, Drew, sashaying to class—but I made sure to avoid him, taking notes from my stepdad's lowering-the-eyes technique when we crossed paths. Now, I stared at Lee's wrist, decorated with expired glow sticks I'd later find out were from nights partying downtown with a fake ID.

"You choopy choopy?" he asked.

They were his first words to me. I looked around hoping he might be talking to somebody else, but we were alone.

"You," he repeated, pantomiming brushing his teeth, "choopy choopy? Sucky sucky?"

It took me a moment to process this. His hand moving

from side to side, his tongue poking his cheek. Sucky sucky? Did he think I didn't speak English? What?

The way he held the toothbrush. Suddenly I realized he wasn't brushing. He was blowing an air-dick.

"I ... no ... sorry, I ... *no,*" I stammered, running out of the closet horrified. As I made my way to the theater, the cast streamed in with snacks from the gas station across the street. I slipped in with the crowd and pretended I'd been with them the whole time so they wouldn't wonder what Lee and I had been doing in there together.

Maybe out of spite, Lee spread the nickname Choopy Choopy around. It caught on. Bianca didn't know it, but by calling out my bad singing and insisting I was like every other boy, she was protecting me. Because of her, I wasn't gay. I just hated women. Thank God.

"Toxically masculine," she'd told Mister when I couldn't harmonize. And when she saw the lengths I went to avoid Lee, pretending I couldn't hear when he spoke to me: "You don't have to be an asshole to him." She was a feminist. An ally before it was cool. And she thought, if she appealed to my humanity, I would see Lee and I had a lot in common.

Bianca's boyfriend, Quist, hung around rehearsals so often that Mister decided to put him in the show. Rumor had it he was in a gang and Mister was trying to rehabilitate him by letting him be in the musical, which is exactly the sort of thing that would happen in a musical. It was easy to see what attracted Bianca to Quist. He had a car, worked full-time at a home-improvement store, and had muscular arms that belonged on a package of industrial-strength toilet paper, flexing assertively. Plus, he was putting his toxic masculinity to good use by helping build our sets.

Not many years before, Congress passed the No Child Left Behind Act, making it the law in Florida that public schools would be funded by how well they performed on state-mandated standardized tests. Because a not-small portion of my classmates were recent immigrants from Haiti, the Dominican Republic, and Puerto Rico and mainly spoke Creole or Spanish, Oak Ridge could never score well on these tests, which were only offered in English. The little money the school received went to the most important things, like golf carts for the campus police. So when Quist showed up with his employee discount on two-by-fours, no one cared that he was twenty years old and technically trespassing. The cast embraced him immediately.

Though Bianca embraced him most. Mid-rehearsal she would call for breaks with some flimsy excuse about having to do a menial task that was suddenly urgent. "I think someone left the back door open!" she'd say, or, "Has anyone checked on the greenroom lights?" As though, if we didn't keep an eye on them, they'd spark an electrical fire and barbecue us alive. When someone would volunteer to check, she'd pull on Quist's hand.

"No, no," she'd scoff and flip her crunchy wet-gel curls. "You won't do it right. We'll take care of it."

Soon, the cast began to disappear into their own Harlequin romances. *The Waitress and the Mailman.* *The Housewife and the Mason.* *The Valet Attendant and the Schoolteacher.*

By the time we were a month into rehearsals, it seemed the only ones who hadn't paired off were me, Angel, and Sad Little Rich Girl, who forgot to go to most rehearsals anyway. When she did make it, reeking of Victoria's Secret body spray and pot, she'd hide behind the curtain, whispering jokes to whoever happened to pass her by.

"Hey, you . . ." she'd call out. "What's brown and sticky?"

Her victim would go through a list of possible answers—worms, hamburger meat, toes—before finally throwing their hands up in defeat and saying the obvious. "Poop. It's poop, isn't it? Ha ha. Very funny."

"No, silly," she'd cackle, pleased that she'd gotten another one of us. "A stick!"

When she eventually quit the musical altogether, the curtain became a make-out spot for the set-design kids. Angel would sit in the auditorium reading his Bible while fingering the gold cross he wore around his neck. Other times, he sang gospel to himself in his Colombian-accented Spanish, songs about how faith had the power to move mountains. No matter what I was doing, when I heard him singing, I'd slide into a nearby seat and pretend to text. His sweet, soulful voice hypnotized me, radiating with an ache that felt both distant and familiar. Bianca was right. Had his voice been coming out of my mouth, I'd have been embarrassed. Perhaps that's what charmed me about him. His certainty that no one would laugh, how freely he expressed his emotions. Within minutes I'd fall into a state similar to sleep. The lyrics about God would drop away, and in my dreams all I heard was the longing underpinning his words, for something else, for more.

Angel and I were waiting at the bus stop for our moms to pick us up, a routine we'd fallen into after rehearsals. We weren't friends. We were more like coworkers. If we spoke, it was usually about the show. Rarely anything that required more than a head nod and an *mm-hmm*. This day, basketball practice let out early, and one of the players on the team joined us. He took a seat on the bench and wiped the sweat off his brow with the bottom of his jersey, letting out a deep sigh we all understood was about the heat. Angel and I nodded and said *mm-hmm*.

A few seconds later I heard a soft, intermittent drumming. I looked up from the textbook spread open on my lap and saw the player spinning a ball on his index finger, occasionally patting it to keep it going. After a while, the ball bored him and he dropped it into his gym bag.

"Yo," he called to us. He cocked his head and squinted as if he were trying to identify what kind of birds we were. Angel with his R&B-singer earrings. My long, curly brown hair. The player smirked, figuring it out. "You drama kids, right?"

Angel shot me a look but stayed quiet. He seemed to be considering whether I would give him up if he lied.

"Yeah," he said, shrugging. "It'll look good on my college application."

The player nodded and propped an immaculate Jordan on top of the basketball. "True. True." Then something else occurred to him. Drama kids weren't just any birds. We were the invasive kind that whistled Judy Garland tunes and decorated our nests with condom wrappers and pages torn from *Good Housekeeping*. "Isn't drama all, like, fags and shit?" he asked.

Angel flinched.

"Not really," I cut in, I don't know why. I could have kept my mouth shut. "But I wouldn't care if it was. I don't have a problem with gay people."

"You don't?" Angel asked.

The player looked equally perplexed.

There was no reason for this to be the right time. A weekday. On a bench with a swastika etched on it in Sharpie. Maybe it was the way Angel reacted to being asked about fags. He didn't get defensive or say, "Yeah, more pussy for me," like some other boys would have.

"Well, you know," I heard myself say. "I'm gay."

What did you do? I thought immediately. You idiot. You can't tell people that. This isn't some online chat room. This is real life. I dropped my eyes back down to my homework, hoping they'd misheard me. Maybe I could pretend I was kidding. Laugh and scream, "Sike! You should have seen your faces!" Before I could do damage control, Angel's body shifted next to mine.

"I think I am too," he said.

The player grabbed his gym bag and waited for his ride down the street.

We didn't need to ask each other; we just were: a couple, on the other side of the closet now, in love. I know the love part sounds fast, but there wasn't any room in my mind for half-baked emotions. If I came out, it had to be for the real thing, the mountain-moving type of devotion. Otherwise we put ourselves at risk for what? Dumb crushes? To be radically honest? Please.

Swept up in that love, I was fascinated by every detail about him. His favorite food (chicken fingers), favorite movie (*Remember the Titans*), what he wanted to be when he grew up (of service). His family was Pentecostal. I read online that Pentecostals spoke in tongues and believed the Bible contained no lies. This might have been a red flag, but I figured religion was how Angel shielded himself: as long as he was singing gospel, his parents wouldn't care that he was singing, which everyone knows is gay.

Angel was curious about me too. Early on, while we were still feeling each other out, he mentioned hearing about my drug record. It was something I vaguely talked about at school with the intention of it adding to my air of mystery. Now, however, I worried that if I didn't clear things up, his imagination would fill in the gaps with something worse than what happened. One day after rehearsal I sat him down in the theater and explained everything as best as I could.

I told him how, in middle school, a man spoke to my class about a law that allowed us to enroll at any public high school as long we provided our own transportation and the new school offered something exceptional that the one we were zoned for didn't. I was zoned for Oak Ridge, but the man said I could attend Boone—one of the best schools in Orlando, where there was a *pool* and students took field trips to Washington—since it had a criminal justice program.

I'd assumed other kids from my block would apply to try to get a better education. My first day there, though, I discovered my classes were instead full of white boys who genuinely wanted to be cops. Most of them didn't even know about the law—they lived near enough to go to Boone whether they'd enrolled in the program or not. The boy next to me smiled eagerly as the program director described the dress code we were expected to follow. Military fatigues and combat boots. No jewelry. No hair past our ears. I was mortified, but it was too late to back out. Mom buzzed my curls off that week and took me to an army surplus store where the director said I could find used boots at a discounted price.

Because Hector was my ride, and he attended a magnet program on the other end of the city, after school I waited hours for him to drive over and take me home. I passed the time walking around the Boone neighborhood. Every house there was beige, the grass on every lawn mowed to one inch or less. More than once I ended up lost and desperate for an identifying marker to guide myself by. On my block, weeds grew tall and blond and houses were all bright primary colors, roofs dripping with Christmas lights well into the summer. Those things that made people call my neighborhood *ghetto* were precisely what made it possible to navigate. If I was proud of that, the feeling went away after a classmate found out where I lived and asked me if I was in a gang.

Halfway through the year I made friends with this white kid named Colton. He invited me over so I wouldn't have to wait for Hector on campus alone. We'd get stoned in his bedroom with pot he bought from a guy I never met, and we'd roll out on our skateboards, fighting back our cottonmouth with dollar cans of Arizona iced tea. At the mall we binged on free food-court samples, then crashed on the display beds at J. C. Penney until the employees yelled at us to leave. Skating around the parking lot with him, I forgot about the strange bald-headed boy I saw in the mirror, Hector's comments about how much he spent on gas shuttling me around, my secret.

Though his parents had money, Colton started dealing.

He was cocky, waving dime bags in the air at lunch and shouting prices like it was a game. I begged him to be more careful, but he wouldn't listen. "Come on, man." He parroted my warnings back in a whiney voice. "This isn't funny." When the campus police caught him, Colton told them we worked together. I don't know why. I can only guess it was to reduce his sentence.

That day, an officer pulled me out of class and took me to a small room with a smaller table, two chairs on each end. He said he had a picture of me selling weed, that two other people I now realize he was making up had named me too, then pushed a paper and pencil in front of me.

I lied and wrote down everything he told me because I didn't think it would make a difference. Because he said if I did, I could leave. Because I wanted to go home and drink coffee and be done, be J.Lo. I even confessed to having weed in my book bag, which was a lie too. The officer never checked, didn't bother to ask for my locker number. Clearly it wasn't the drugs that were the problem, or he'd have confiscated them; the problem was me.

Before sophomore year began, Mom and I met with the superintendent, a person of color who I felt more comfortable telling the truth to. I'm not sure what convinced him I wasn't lying. Maybe it was my good grades, or that I cried when I told him I was afraid I'd never get into college. For whatever reason, he wiped the expulsion from my record, giving me a fresh start at the place I'd always belonged, Oak Ridge. Colton's family enrolled him in a private Catholic school.

"God works in mysterious ways," Angel said, looking on at the dark, empty stage.

"Yeah." I leaned my head on his shoulder. "Imagine, if I hadn't gotten kicked out, I would have never met you."

We took things slow. First, holding hands, his palms cold and damp against mine. I thought it was sweet that I made him sweat. Between classes we passed each other elaborately folded notes. Origami swans with "Miss you, boo" written in their bellies. Boats full of hearts. I especially loved that he was a little chubby. That meant he didn't deny himself what made him happy, and what made him happy, the fleet of love boats I arranged on my windowsill proved, was me. At night I curled up on the couch scrolling through pictures of him on my cell phone, high off the dimple on his chin, his full, pink lips. It took me a week to notice that Mom accidentally set the DVR to record every episode of one of her novelas, erasing all my rom-coms. I didn't care. I didn't need them anymore.

When we finally kissed, me on my tiptoes, hidden behind the red velvet curtain onstage, our teeth clanged against each other's like chopsticks before a meal. I wanted Angel three times a day. We practiced. Sitting. Kneeling. Me standing on an apple crate.

Office Worker #1 and Office Worker #3.

It was almost too perfect. Corny as hell, but I devoured it. I could taste that wedding on a boat.

A few times, I opened my eyes to double-check I wasn't making him up. Once, I found him staring back. We kept going, eyes wide, neither of us certain who had caught whom.

I knew why I was peeking, but why was he?

I tried not to read into it. Don't be paranoid, I told myself. You used to think someone would try to kill you if you came out, and you've never felt so alive.

Bianca began to share her cereal with me at rehearsals. Quist helped me with my falsetto. Lee came around too. Now that

I wasn't in the closet, he wanted to be my "gay mentor," like on the TV show *Queer Eye for the Straight Guy*, which he said he planned on auditioning for as soon as he turned eighteen. In retrospect, his advice could have been useful to anyone, gay or otherwise.

"First off," he told me, "you really have to stop telling people you don't poop."

He taught me what to wear: "Not that." Cool clubs where I could go if I got a fake ID: "Hank's is for old people. Parliament House has the best drinks. You like Long Islands, right?" What to say when some guy asked what it felt like to have a dick up my ass, though Angel and I hadn't moved beyond kissing: "Why, are you curious?"

If that didn't work, I had backup. For every jock who called me a maricón, there was a cheerleader armed with words that cut deeper than their pointed nail files.

"Leave that boy alone," they said. "What are you, obsessed with him?"

In return I told them they looked fierce, fly, fabulous, barking out so many compliments I earned a seat in class on their laps. Messing with me became like kicking a girl's dog.

Just once, a group of boys followed me around campus. I was late to class and alone.

"Faaaa . . ." one said, stretching the word out.

I couldn't tell how many of them were behind me. I kept my pace steady, unbothered.

". . . got 'em," he finished, then laughed at his own joke.

Another voice cracked up.

"Deadass, dog likes to get fucked up the booty," a third joined in. "That's messed up."

"Don't be nasty. Now I got visuals and shit."

"Faaaa . . ."

I dug through my messenger bag until I found a pen, curled my fingers around its spine. I wasn't sure I would need it. I wasn't sure I wouldn't. Where were the teachers? Damn, where were the administrators? This broke-ass school couldn't afford shit. I turned around to get it over with. And then, registering their faces, my fingers loosened around the pen.

They were boys I went to elementary school with. Boys from my neighborhood. We'd gone on field trips to Universal Studios together, stuffed our sneakers with toilet paper in the bathroom so we'd be tall enough to get on the Incredible Hulk ride. All of a sudden I realized I didn't need a good comeback, only the awkward truth: I wasn't some random gay guy on TV they could laugh at from a distance. We knew each other.

"Didn't your mom give me a ride home once?" I almost asked. "Doesn't *yours* sell flan at church?"

Instead I simply stood there, caught between wanting to remind them that we used to be friends and daring them to try something. Eventually we parted ways, all of us looking uncomfortable.

It wasn't until our AP Government teacher staged a mock debate in class that I understood the line I walked at Oak Ridge.

The topic: Should gay couples be allowed to adopt children?

"Raise your hand if you're in favor," he ordered the class.

Mine went up eagerly, then wavered in the air as I gradually noticed everyone else had remained still. I looked at the girls in class for support. On the subject of me and children, they found other places to stare. Even Manny Rivera, who used an old Crown Royal bag to hold his school supplies, thought he had more of a right to be a father than me.

"Look, I don't care if someone's gay," he said. "But you gotta think about the kids and how people are gonna treat them in school. Those kids are gonna get bullied." He frowned. "That's not cool, man."

We were having lunch the first time Angel mentioned Lee being too gay. I was drinking my box milk with the skinny pink straw it came with.

"Lee powders his face in class," Angel said. "Weird, right?"

I slipped the straw out of my mouth.

"Dude. You can be gay without being *gay*," he went on. A friend of a friend told him that Lee's boyfriend, Drew, shoved shampoo bottles up his butt to prepare himself for sex. I liked Lee, but I loved Angel. Beneath the table, he trailed a finger over the top of my hand. It'd been almost two months since we started dating, and his touch still made my neck tingle.

"Whoa," I replied. "Yeah, that *is* weird."

Even though people mostly left me and Angel alone, boys like Drew, who wore a rainbow puka shell necklace everywhere, were asking for it. You can be gay without being *gay* was more than a theory; it was a rule. No one was shocked when Drew got jumped walking home from school one afternoon. Neither of us knew the exact details. It was easier to stop listening and tell ourselves we were exempt, do what we had to do to keep it that way.

And what I had to do, Angel told me, was cut my hair. It was getting too long.

That night I sat on the toilet, my head poking through a black garbage bag.

I wasn't uncommonly insecure, but I wasn't thrilled about my appearance either. I was short, with the kind of acne that hurt, and half my clothes were stained because I bit my fingernails so much they bled. I did, however, like my curls. They made me look like Shakira when she was punk and only performed barefoot. Drew had shown up to school the day after he'd been supposedly attacked the same as usual. He acted normal enough, though he broke up with Lee and didn't have his rainbow necklace on anymore. I didn't know what to believe.

"You sure you want me to do this?" Mom asked, scissors at the ready.

I wasn't. But I wanted to make Angel happy. I sobbed as my hair drizzled around me.

"I didn't realize your ears were so . . . big," he said when

I showed him the haircut on campus the next day. It was true. My hair used to fall over my ears. Now I looked like I was wearing flesh earmuffs. He cupped them in his hands. My fat ears burned inside his palms. "Were they always like this?"

Angel let me borrow his hoodie to cover them. In class, I buried my face in the sleeves, inhaling the lingering Axe body spray in the fabric, thankful that I had a boyfriend who would literally give me the clothes off his back.

He told me we needed to start being more careful. His older sister, who'd graduated the year before, still had friends at Oak Ridge, and he was worried that word would get to her about me. That could never happen. His parents might find out. He would die.

"I don't know what we were thinking," he said. "Let's chill out a bit, okay?"

I swooned. He couldn't risk us. That's how badly he wanted to be with me.

So we stopped holding hands. No more notes. No paper trail. Nothing to see here. When I'd slide in beside him at lunch, he'd shove his book bag between our thighs. Then we stopped sitting together completely. I found another place to get picked up after rehearsal so his mom wouldn't see us together. If we passed each other between classes, he kept his eyes glued in front of him. As soon as I made it into a room, heart pounding, I'd burst out laughing. We'd fooled everyone. I felt like a cartoon robber pulling off a heist.

"What's so funny?" my classmates would ask. I'd be

giggling to myself, thinking about how much truer our love was because we had to keep it a secret. We were like *Romeo and Juliet. The Wedding Planner.* Better. Those were fake.

"I don't know," I'd say, smug. "What's brown and sticky?"

I think I have a crush on someone else.

I was washing dishes when my phone vibrated with Angel's text. I read it quickly, then plunged the phone back into my jeans. A greasy pan waited in the sink for me to scrape clean. Calm down, I thought. Don't get ahead of yourself. This isn't that bad yet.

I reached for a sponge and began working on the pan, watching it go from black to brown to its original silver. It was satisfying to watch a problem be solved so easily. I grabbed the next dish, took a deep breath, let my mind drift away into our rom-com.

Office Worker #3. Office Worker #1. We were meant for each other. It didn't make sense for there to be "someone else." I came out to *him*. He loved *me*.

So no. So he was testing me. So that had to be it. In every rom-com, there's one last test. After the couple has fallen in love, the universe throws a ticking clock (*The Holiday*) or a sprinkle of short-term memory loss (*50 First Dates*) into their plans. Before was the rom part; this was the com, when the audience watches the new couple fumble to remain together despite these seemingly impossible challenges. If they can beat their tests, their love is real.

Ours was classic: I was supposed to let him go so he could see how badly he missed me.

I dropped the sponge and fished my phone back out.

Okay, I wrote. *If you like someone else, don't let me stop you.*

I pictured him receiving my message, how floored he'd be by my selflessness, how cool he'd think I was. He'd realize he'd been an idiot to even look at another boy and spend the rest of the year desperately trying to win me back. There would be grand gestures. I knew a kid who did tattoos out of his dad's garage. Or he could take me to The Cheesecake Factory.

Thanks, he wrote back.

The next morning, Lee picked me up in his car before school. While I waited for us to take off, he removed a joint from his shirt pocket. I hadn't smoked since I started at Oak Ridge— the possibility of getting expelled again terrified me. But I wanted a quick distraction, so I took it. We pulled out onto the road, taking hits, blowing smoke out the window. My insides grew warm and fuzzy, like they were being embraced by an old friend.

"Fuck," he said as we drove by campus. "I can't with this place today. Let's do something. Let's go somewhere."

When we arrived at the nearby movie theater, no one was manning the ticket stand. We walked in anyway and opened the door to an empty auditorium. Inside, I stood on a seat in the back row and peeked into the projector room. It was empty too. We didn't know what movie they were playing, whether they would show one at all.

Sitting beside him in the dark, I told Lee about my theory. How even though Angel claimed to have a crush and had been avoiding me, we were obviously meant for each other. I knew since he sat next to me at that first rehearsal. It was all so romantic, if you thought about it.

"Oh, girl," he laughed. "How much did you smoke?"

I crossed my arms and glared ahead at the clear white screen.

"Whatever," I said. "You don't get it."

Before he could respond, the lights dimmed and the title of the movie appeared. *Body of Lies*. An action film. Lee and I looked at each other and giggled our disappointment away. As the images of car chases and shoot-outs flickered onscreen, I laid my head on his shoulder, too stoned to follow the plot.

What if he's right? I wondered.

Lee was older, had more experience. Was I crazy?

I breathed in his cozy laundry-detergent smell, breaking down Angel's text message in my head piece by piece. He had a crush on someone else. He liked them enough to tell me. He liked them enough to jeopardize what we had. I repeated those three things over and over until only the worst part remained: he had a crush on someone else.

The only evidence that he ever even had a crush on *me* was some folded-up paper wilting on my windowsill. It suddenly felt so simple. I suddenly felt so simple. And pathetic.

The minutes rolled by without Lee pushing me off. His fingertip pirouetted on my elbow, drawing something confusing out of me. Not desire, exactly. Gratitude? At least he was honest. At least he didn't let me humiliate myself. Wasn't that a kind of love, if not the one I wanted? I moved my hand down his jeans. His crotch stiffened against my palm. I waited to see if he'd brush me off. When a few seconds passed and he still hadn't, I cleared a space among the popcorn kernels on the floor with my feet, then dropped to my knees and lowered his zipper. His head fell back as I reached inside to pull out his dick. A single translucent drop sat on the tip. I licked it, wincing through the saltiness, and inserted the rest into my mouth.

In the background, people talked on and on in hushed, secretive tones, followed by more gun shots, more tires screeching, the same tired story. Boys being boys.

"I'm close," Lee finally said.

I lifted my head. "To what?"

"Where do you want me to come?"

I looked around the seats. There wasn't anywhere he could do it that someone wouldn't have to clean. I pointed at my tongue. His eyes widened. I dove back in, squeezing the side of his seat for support. Less than a minute later my mouth filled up, and I was warm again inside. I swallowed quickly, stood up, and sat back down next to him. We watched the rest of the movie in silence, neither of us acknowledging what had just happened.

What happened is Jennifer Lopez would have never

given a guy a blow job in an empty movie theater. What happened is Angel and I were through.

The night of the musical, everyone in the cast huddled around in the greenroom waiting for the show to begin. Angel sat by the water fountain, folding and unfolding the corners of his script. It'd been a week since we'd last spoken, and I still didn't know who his crush was. Without anyone to compare myself to, I could only blame the breakup on me: I was too gay, too short. I shouldn't have told him about my record. I shouldn't have let him convince me to cut my hair.

Mister poked his head into the greenroom to let us know we'd be on in five. Through the open door I heard the chatter of people in the auditorium. Half the school was out there. Maybe he was also out there, this new prince charming with his perfect infant ears Angel couldn't get enough of. That gave me an idea.

I opened my cell phone and pressed it to my cheek, pretending to listen for a minute before saying, "Oh shut up, babe!" I leaned back in my chair so my bulge would be on display, then added: "Oh my God, stop, *you* are!" In my peripheral vision, Angel craned his neck to listen to me talk to my amazing fake boyfriend. "Thanks for coming. You're the sweetest. You really didn't have to do that!" I stood up and breezed past him on my way toward the water fountain, then thrust my ass out and bent over for a drink. "You're right.

You *did* owe me. Third row? Okay, I'll try to find you, but I'm not really supposed to look. Definitely see you after though."

"Edgar . . ." The sound of Angel's voice reached around my waist.

I snapped my phone shut and turned around.

Angel looked from the floor to his hands to my face. "You're seeing someone?"

"Oh, yeah, it's new. He goes to Boone. How are you and . . . ?"

"Me and who?" he said. Just like that. Just like he hadn't dumped me days before precisely so there could be a him and a who. He spun a silver ring around his finger. "Oh, I'm not . . . I'm not dating anyone. I'm saving myself. For marriage."

I blinked.

"To a girl," he went on, in case I didn't get it. He showed me the ring. The engraving of a cross that reminded him to stay pure. He'd made a vow. With God. Like he and God had talked about me and none of it was good. Angel read my mind: The crush? Made up. He figured it'd be easier to lie. It was too much to explain, and I wouldn't understand. "Anyway, you got a man now!" he said and actually laughed. "So, I guess, um, yeah. Good luck."

I blinked again.

We were onstage. The Waitress's number. Angel and I played a couple dining in her restaurant. I sat across from him reading a prop menu. Mister had instructed us to mouth words to each other so it'd look to the audience like we were having a conversation.

"The fish looks good," Angel said. It was our first and last public date.

I squeezed my menu tighter, trying to summon the energy to act. "I'm talking to you," I mouthed back. "I'm talking to you. We are two people talking."

In the audience, flashes went off. I imagined Angel's family sitting there—his sister, his mom, his dad holding a camera up. What they were seeing playing out onstage. A teenage girl belting, "It's an art! It's an art!" while twirling plates in her hands. In the background, two boys saying nothing to each other, one of them wishing he could ask:

Did I do something wrong?

Does any part of you miss me?

Do you know, if you wanted, I would have kept on hiding for us?

It wasn't romantic. Or funny. But there was enough truth in that to help me believe one last lie, at least until The Waitress stopped singing and I could run backstage. The lie was that if he could be who he wanted to be, if his family weren't watching, he'd flip the table over, lift me in his arms, carry me behind the curtain to our happy ending. Right now he was just following someone's stage directions. There was a voice whispering into his ear. He was under its control.

Smile! the voice said. Another flash lit up the auditorium.

"The chicken looks good," Angel mouthed.

Laugh!
"We are talking."
Now a serious one.
"We are talking."
Put on a straight face.

Mama's Boy

This commercial is so good they played it in movie theaters. It opens with a starlet being chased by paparazzi through Times Square in New York. The train of her gown billows behind her like a cape, shielding her pale white face from an assault of camera flashes. She dives into the nearest cab, slamming the door shut. Only then does she realize there's a man in the back seat with her.

We hear him in voice-over. "I must have been the only person who didn't know who she was," he says with a foreign accent, though it's so obvious. She's the most famous woman in the world. A perfect blond curl dangles irresistibly from her forehead. His lips are soft and wet. These things make the two of them mad with horniness.

"Drive!" she yells at the man behind the wheel.

Fast-forward and now she and the mysterious passenger

are dancing on a rooftop. "It's beautiful up here," she says. "Everything seems so peaceful."

"Who are you?" he asks, and then he dips her. Kisses her. Fireworks burst behind them, smearing the sky with their cum.

In the end we see her walking a red carpet, the plunging neckline of her dress exposing the pink slope of her back, where a diamond pendant hangs from a necklace. Sparkles reflecting off it beckon toward the man, who is still on the rooftop, watching. She turns around and smiles, assuring him she hasn't forgotten. He hasn't forgotten her either: not her kisses, or the times they spent together with her body folded into his, and never her perfume: Chanel No. 5.

Miguel didn't want to be a girl. He wanted to be like that.

Around nine o'clock each night, he'd park his car at the end of my block and send a text message: *Come out, come out.* Already dressed in my tightest jeans and a hoodie, I'd press my ear to my bedroom door to make sure the coast was clear. In the bathroom across the hall, the sound of drumming water would let me know my stepdad was taking his fourth or fifth shower of the day. We still didn't speak, but I assumed this latest obsession had something to do with him emptying his liquor bottles down the drain months back and turning his life over to Christ. Further away, in the living room, I'd invariably hear Mom scolding the characters in her novelas. María Hernández can't live with her secret any longer, but she must, but she can't, but she *must*. "Oh, shut up," Mom groaned. "This girl, every little thing has to be a big drama!" At the first gunshot or *DUN DUN DUN*, I'd lock the door, throw my book bag out my window, and run.

A minute later I'd climb into Miguel's sun-bleached Honda Civic with a broken rearview mirror that hung like a dangly earring. The Speed Queen, he called it. We'd drive off blasting Whitney Houston. Her latest album, *I Look to You*, stayed playing on the stereo. While I flattened that day's homework against the passenger window, filling out my AP Biology worksheets by moonlight, he'd lip-sync along to his favorite track, "Million Dollar Bill."

"What's cartilage for?" I'd ask him. Or, "If you have green eyes, and your wife has brown eyes, what color eyes will your kids have?"

"If he makes you feel like a million-dollar bill, say it!" he'd answer, dancing in his seat. The moon was more helpful.

At his apartment, we'd work on the night's look. "Put on that gay shit," he'd command, my cue to snatch *Mean Girls* or *Breakfast at Tiffany's* from his bookshelf for us to watch as I painted the bottoms of his high heels with red nail polish and he hot-glued rhinestones to his fishnets.

Once his wig was in place—he only owned one, a wilted Shake-N-Go from the Magic Mall in the style CHOCO#2B that we took turns teasing and spraying into a bouncy, curly cloud—I was supposed to start calling him by his drag name, Princess.

We'd head out to his "gigs." These were performances at amateur nights where he was paid up to nineteen dollars in tips. Other times he simply showed up to a club done up for the free drinks, and I stuck to his back to avoid the under-twenty-one cover. We'd pick a corner of the dance floor and wait, the swirling LED lights licking our faces as we scrolled through the headless torsos on Grindr and tried to match them to the sweaty boys around us.

On their way to the bar, these same boys who ignored Miguel's messages stopped to take us in. Their bloodshot eyes widened at the sight of so many sequins, of CHOCO#2B, not onstage or on *Jerry Springer*, but close enough for them to reach out and touch. A real Princess.

"Do you mind?" they asked, thrusting their phones at me. "Hold it like this. Press here. Take a couple."

"I got it," I said.

Princess arranged their hands on her breasts, stole a sip from their cocktails.

I'd count down. Three, two, and then the club—whichever we were at—would light up for half a second before returning to dark. Seeing the flash, more people would gather around to find out what the big fuss was about. They'd look at me in my boring clothes, at all of Princess's sparkles, and I could practically feel their interest in me waning. I wasn't offended. It was a relief. I loved that no one cared who I was, that no one was angry at me, or sad, or disappointed. Hidden inside my friend's glow, I didn't have to be anything, because Princess was everything.

•

Two freshman girls made out at some jock's birthday party, with tongue, and neither of them had drunk more than a few Smirnoffs. You didn't have to be there. Talk of the kiss rolled through the cafeteria gathering details—their eyes were *closed*; no wonder they kept their nails short—pushed on by the same kids who, two years earlier, claimed I'd tried to turn Angel gay.

Choopy Choopy, people at school still called me senior year. Sucky Sucky. The rumor was that if I kissed you, you'd catch it, whatever Angel was infected with that made him change his braces to the colors of the rainbow one day and lead morning prayer circle around the flagpole the next. After we broke up, he couldn't stick to being gay or straight longer than a month. I heard it was my fault enough for the lie to stop sounding crazy. Any rumor, heard twice, loses its novelty, becomes familiar. I did that to him. I was contagious.

Lee, who'd graduated and moved to New York, told me to mind my business when I texted him about the girls. His general attitude about them and Angel was that it was all very *high school*. Once I left Oak Ridge I wouldn't remember any of their names, he said. In the meantime, he suggested I try to have as much fun as I could before I had real problems, like rent.

It was Gay Pride weekend, so that Saturday, I rode the city bus to the parade with a flask of guava wine—the only alcohol we had left at home—shoved into my underwear. It wasn't my first Pride, but it was my first one alone. I wondered if the other people seated around me had any idea where I was going in my little denim shorts and tank top.

Once there, I followed the sound of upbeat music to a street overflowing with gay people. I found a spot among them and watched the trans elders marching with their fists in the air, the go-go boys hurling condoms from the tops of floats, the Dykes on Bikes pressing on the horns of their motorcycles, leaving in their wake a road littered with beads and confetti. I tried to match everyone's energy, but it felt awkward to smile and scream by myself, like I was crashing a party and they all knew. I wasn't even sure what I was supposed to be proud of.

The closest thing was this: the year before, I came out to my mom.

We'd been at the Clinique counter inside Saks Fifth Avenue, waiting to ask an employee about a coupon we'd gotten in the mail. There was no good reason for me to do it then, like there hadn't been one when I'd told Angel. I suppose I just wanted to get it over with, and my gut told me she wouldn't make a scene around so many rich white ladies.

"I have to tell you something," I said, laying it out as gently as if I were dropping the words into hot oil: "I think I like boys. I think I'm gay."

"Okay," Mom said, and then she put on her sunglasses, I guessed to cry. I was getting ready for her to grab my arm and pull me out of the store when a salesgirl came up to us and offered her some free samples. Mom smiled and acted as if nothing had just happened. Maybe I should have thought it was strange how quickly the moment passed, and a part of me did, but mostly I was focused on the fact that, seconds later, she'd moved on and was buying me a three-month supply of face wash. That's it? I thought. It was such a nice idea that I let myself believe it: she really doesn't care.

It wasn't until we made it back home and I heard her sobbing on the phone with an aunt that I understood how badly I'd hurt her. I expected my aunt would talk some sense into her and when she finished the call she'd come into my room and kick me out or whoop me. But she didn't. She didn't do a thing. I was so grateful, I got it in my head that I could repay her for her acceptance by proving that my being gay didn't mean I was going to change. If she waited a little, I'd show her I was practically still straight. Within a week I hung up a Miami Dolphins football calendar in my room, threw out all my rom-coms, packed my flamboyant clothes into a suitcase and hid it under my bed. In retrospect this must have only confused her. It confused me. After all, what was the point of coming out if I was just going to re-closet myself?

Standing on the side of the street at Pride, surrounded by queers who seemed way more fearless than I could ever be, I felt like a poser. I ducked inside a Porta Potty and swallowed the flask of guava wine in one gulp, gagging at the toilet stench flooding my nostrils. The graffiti-tagged walls were slimy with humidity, the space cramped and dark, but I was more comfortable in there than outside. It was easier to breathe with no one watching.

When someone knocked on the door, I summoned the nerve to open it by promising myself I could leave in an hour. There was a strip of sidewalk nearby where businesses had set up booths selling rainbow sunglasses and giving free rapid HIV tests. I made my way over and tried looking available by standing near groups of strangers and laughing. Some of them, mainly older men wearing western shirts tucked into Wranglers, played along. *Pride is so corporate now*, they said, and *Smile! What do you have to be sad about? When I was your age—phew!*

I accepted greedily. Their attention. The vodka cranberries and tequila sunrises they offered.

They moved in closer, rubbed my chest through my clothes, squeezed my ass. *Where do you live?* They pulled me between their legs, slobbered on my neck. *How old are you?*

With my mom, I answered, wiping their spit off my skin. Almost eighteen.

By nightfall, I'd lost my flask and was holding on to someone's sticky hand. I didn't know who they were, or how we'd pushed past thousands of bodies to the front of the free Lisa Lisa concert. The man gradually came into focus as I sobered up: he was short, and bald, with chubby, pockmarked cheeks that looked like the gum center of a Blow Pop. Maybe I was still drunk, I thought, because as much as I blinked, his eyebrows never appeared. In the hand not holding mine he carried a plastic cup. He must have been old enough to buy himself alcohol, though his outfit—an oversized Lady Gaga T-shirt and leggings—made me think he

couldn't have been over twenty-three. He waved his drink in
the air to Lisa Lisa. We were, apparently, talking.

"... can't just get in a car with anyone," he was saying.
"Este lugar está lleno de locos. Bitch, you have nice skin.
Do you get that a lot? What is that, NC ... 40 ... 42?
No, they're foundation shades. MAC. I'm a makeup artist.
Oh, girl, no, don't use drugstore. That shit'll make you break
out. I can get you a discount. I'll hook it up. Can I tell you
a secret? I don't know this song. Don't laugh! I don't know
this lady. Do you? Stop laughing! Who is this? Yeah, totally,
mom music. Wanna go to Parliament House? I'm over her.
She's cute but this song is killing my vibe. I want Whitney.
Stop, she is *not* mom music! Come on, let's go, I can get you
in for free."

Parliament House was packed shoulder to shoulder with
the runoff from Pride. The man—who introduced himself as Miguel on the ride over—and I burrowed our way
through the dance floor to the massive outdoor courtyard,
where hundreds of shirtless dudes who had the same idea as
us shook their asses to the techno music pouring out of the
club. String lights suspended from palm trees crisscrossed
the dark purple sky, waving in the breeze. In my tipsy haze
they looked like lightning bugs. I was in love.

"Damn, I forgot this place sucks," Miguel said.

No one else seemed to think so. Everywhere people were
kissing and grinding up against each other or taking selfies

with a seven-foot-tall drag queen dripping with rainbow beads.

Miguel noticed me ogling. "You know, all the queens here have AIDS," he said, reading my face for a reaction.

I shoved my hands into my jeans and crushed an acorn into the ground. He seemed satisfied with that, like he'd told this story before and it was one of the acceptable responses.

"They walk around poking people with needles," he went on.

"What the fuck?" I asked, searching the queen's hands for something sharp and reflective, but also careful not to appear too nervous. I didn't want him to take me home yet. "Why would they do that?"

He shrugged. "Why does anyone do anything? Wanna play bingo?"

"Like, now?"

He grabbed my elbow and pushed us out of the crowd, leading me to a fluorescent-lit two-story building that wrapped around the entire edge of the courtyard. It was punctuated with navy-blue doors, most of them closed. Between each one was a floor-to-ceiling window that revealed the motel room inside like a museum display.

"Parliament House bingo," Miguel clarified.

I might have been surprised that a gay club would have its own motel, but in Orlando everything is theme-park sized. In less than an hour I'd counted three dance floors, passed a full-service restaurant, a porn shop, another store that sold antiques, and was invited to a boat party on the private beach while in line for the bathroom, though later I'd find out the "beach" was really just a swamp bordered with sand they'd trucked in from somewhere else.

We climbed the stairs to the second-floor motel balcony. Leaning against the waist-high railing, I watched the tightly packed bodies gyrating below. The space where Miguel and I had been standing just a second ago had been immediately filled by two new men wearing neon short shorts. One stretched his tongue out of his mouth, like he was catching snowflakes, and the other placed a tiny white square on the tip. They threw their arms around each other, then laughed at the vast, endless sky, as if there were a funny memory playing up there that only they could see. I suspected that if they walked away, two more men would descend from above to replace them, like pigeons tagging out on a telephone wire. It was bizarre, looking down at everyone, to think that at school I was such a freak, when here the only thing remarkable about me was that I wasn't on Molly, or stabbing people. There was something to be proud of.

"You know it's rude to stare," Miguel called from behind me.

I spun around. "I wasn't."

"Is this your first time at Pee House?"

Yes. Obviously, yes. "No," I said. "They have the best Long Islands here."

"Long Islands? Messy." He approached one of the motel-room windows and cupped his hands against it, then leaned in. His lips curled into a smile. "B," he said. He peeled himself off, leaving a ring of condensation on the glass. "Come look."

There was a playful sweetness to his bright green eyes, like split-open kiwis, that made me think whatever he wanted me to see would be good for me, or at least fun.

I moved beside him, following his gaze through the window, past the mustard-colored room curtains, which were parted several inches, to a bed. It took me a second to untangle the legs and backs and arms I saw twisting into one another, then the picture sorted itself out. Three men. Fucking.

"Oh my God," I said, stepping back. "Do they know we can see?"

"Duh. They want people to. Check the lock. The door's open so, like, anyone can join." Miguel made having an orgy sound so common, no different from passing a bakery and deciding to get one of the donuts on display.

"You get a letter every time you see something weird," he explained.

"Oh," I said, and took another look. "What counts as weird?"

One of the men fell to his stomach and slid a pillow under it. The two others moved in front and behind him. His mouth fell open as the first dick went in.

"You'll know when you see it," he said.

"Well, what happens when we get bingo?"

"Girl," he scoffed. "This ain't Monopoly. Who cares?"

At the next window, the curtains were pulled tight. I grabbed the doorknob and, before I could convince myself not to, twisted it. It clicked—locked. The door to the room after that, though, was open. No one was in there. Cargo shorts lay abandoned on the ragged carpet, a pair of briefs still tucked into them, as if the person wearing the clothes had suddenly been raptured.

We sat on the bed. I ran my fingers along the stiff covers. They were a tacky floral-print pattern, the shadows of old stains blossoming among the leaves. I wondered what it would be like for a man to press my face to them. The thought that someone might stand outside and watch, then walk away like it was nothing, unnerved me. Who lived like this?

"Nice," Miguel said. He'd found the remote control and landed on a channel on the TV. "They have cable."

"Let's move in," I said. I wasn't joking. Anywhere would be better than Mom's house. Everything there was always broken. The toilet flooded weekly. The air conditioner hissed at our attempts to run it. A leak in our roof grew wider with each thunderstorm. Mom sprayed the black mold on our bathroom ceiling with bleach and simply warned me to not stay in there too long. The more we tried to keep things together, the harder it was to ignore that everything was falling apart. I was sick of pretending we weren't poor, of pretending I was straight, of the part-time job I got at Auntie Anne's Pretzels at the mall, where I barely made enough to pay my phone bill, and of the way people looked at me on my breaks when I wore my smelly, baggy uniform into stores. If I could stay here forever, I would.

Parliament House was like a little town. Miguel and I could wake up at noon every morning, eat maraschino cherries for breakfast, bathe at the private beach, brunch like rich white bitches at the restaurant. At night, we'd shake the sand out of our hair on the dance floor and fall asleep in our beds to the sound of house music playing in the courtyard. Just describing to him what our lives could be, it was as if we'd already lived them, and instantly I skipped to the part where we were best friends.

"All right." He set the remote down. "Let's move in."

We watched TV together, the picture brown at the edges.

"I don't have cancer, you know," he said after a while.

"Cool?" I answered. "Me neither."

"Everyone thinks I do because of my eyebrows. Or that I was burned or something. I do drag. It takes like an hour to cover them up with glue, so I just shaved them off to save time."

He showed me a picture on his phone. What were apple cheeks and a double chin on the man beside me were soft, round features on Princess. His fat chest was squeezed into a tight top that shaped it into a pair of porn-star breasts. All the things that made people ignore him as a boy were what made him a beautiful woman. Drag was like magic. It made problems disappear.

"Is it hard?" I asked. "I can help. If you want."

"It can be," he said. "Do you dance? I need dancers."

I did in drama club, before the program was shut down after Mr. King was accused of molesting a student. The case was dismissed, but Miguel didn't need to know all that.

"A little."

"Are you good with makeup?"

"I used to draw horses," I answered.

He didn't seem convinced.

"But I can iron," I added quickly. "And clean your shoes. Heels. Whatever. Whatever you need me to do. Just think about it. It'll be fun." Saying that, too, made it like we were already having it. The fun. "Come on. Think about how much more time you'll have."

"All right, all right," he said, laughing. "Let's go before these people come back."

Mom was seated at the kitchen table when I came home from school, her hands wrapped around a cup of tea, loaded to the brim, no steam. The label hung off the rim like getaway rope.

"Are you a faggot?" she asked before the front door had fully closed behind me.

"What?" I heard the word leave my throat, but the sound belonged to someone else, someone who practiced several takes before landing on this calm, measured version of it.

"I said, are you a faggot?" She stood up, and with a flick of her wrist she swiped the cup of tea to the ground, smashing it into a dozen little pieces. I'd be stepping on them for days, each time the ceramic pierced my feet a reminder that this really happened. One day Mom turned into a novela character.

A pool of brown liquid spread across the tile floor and formed a moat around her Chinese slippers, soaking the hem of the leopard-print house dress she always changed into after work. I didn't know what to do. My mind spun a wheel. Sit down? Cry? Call for help? But who? It landed on *laugh*. A snort escaped my mouth.

She couldn't be serious. We'd already done this. That day at the mall. She'd said okay. None of the articles I'd read online about coming out warned me that after telling my mom I was gay, she might ask me if I was gay.

But I *knew* it'd been too easy. I *knew* it wasn't okay. I *knew* she wasn't one of those "as long as my kid is happy" moms.

"I . . . ," I said softly. "What are you talking about?" I searched her face for a reason she was dredging this up now, and in that moment discovered I hadn't seen her, really seen her, in months. Her copper-tinted hair was greasy and slicked wild, dark roots coming in like weeds. One of her eyes twitched—though it always did, a remnant from a stroke she had years earlier. It was the other eye that scared me. How open it was, focused, even more noticeable because of the puffy bags underneath. She looked like she'd been run over by a bus, or something much worse: the realization that I wasn't going through a phase. But why now?

"Who is this?" she shoved my cell phone in my face. I'd looked everywhere for it that morning. I don't know how she'd gotten it. But that didn't matter. What did was that she had seen my lock screen, which I'd set to a picture of me and Miguel. No, not Miguel. Princess. Our faces pressed together so tightly her long curly hair blended into mine.

"You wanna be a girl?" she asked in English—that way nothing would get lost in translation.

I stopped laughing. This wasn't funny anymore.

"No." I directed my answer at the puddle beneath her feet. "That's just my friend."

She smoothed out the wrinkles on her nightgown and sat down at the table, sighed into her squeezed-together palms, stayed there for a second, then stood up again. "But you're a faggot."

I understood, finally, what it was to be ambushed by that fact. I did what I imagine she wanted to at Saks, when all she could do was hide behind her sunglasses. I ran to my room, slammed the door shut, and turned the lock.

From underneath my bed covers, I heard her slippers approaching. She knocked.

"Let me in."

I wrapped my blanket tight over my head, rocking myself, and for some reason I couldn't explain then, warm in my cocoon, I felt relieved. Deep down I must have known this wouldn't happen a third time. Whatever she said or did next would be the end of it; then we could move on with the rest of our lives. I just had to get through this day. Five minutes at a time.

"Let me in," she said again. The knocking turned to pounding, first concentrated in one spot, where her fist hit.

Then the entire door began to rattle, and I knew she wasn't using her hands anymore; she was coming at it with her body. "Open . . ." My bedframe shook with each blow. "This . . ." A living thing on its knees. "Door!" Trying to crawl away.

"Open this maldita fucking puerta! This is my house! I will not have locked doors!"

"I'm changing!" I screamed. The pounding intensified. I heard it after the wood cracked, after the doorknob toppled out, after the hinges tore out of the wall. Mom crashed into the room, but I could still hear it. Suddenly I realized the pounding was coming from my chest.

As Mom stood in the doorway, huffing, I pressed my hand to my heart to calm it.

You should have known this would happen, I thought. How could you be so careless? So stupid?

Her breathing died down until the room was silent. I wondered if she'd gone, though I didn't dare move the blanket from my face and check. Maybe she thought I was sleeping. It wasn't impossible.

I was beginning to believe that ridiculous lie when the weight of the bed shifted.

"I'm sorry," she said, crawling in. "I love you. My baby. I'm sorry. Perdoname. I didn't mean it. I'm sorry. I love you. My baby." Her arms wrapped around my chest. "Te quiero. Perdon. Lo hice sin querer." I felt her heartbeat slow down to a steady pace against my back, her lips kiss my neck. "I love you. I love you. Te quiero. Perdoname. ¿Me perdonas?" Novela Mom was gone.

I didn't want to forgive her, even if I did, even as I did.
How long had she been sitting there like that before I came
home?

On my eighteenth birthday, Princess and I went to a bar
called Pulse. It was a few blocks from Boone. Hector and I
used to drive by it on the way to school. Because of the white
picket fence surrounding the building, I'd always assumed it
was someone's house.

It was a different kind of home, I discovered, as Princess and I passed through the beaded curtain separating
the front lobby from the dance floor. Her shimmery sequin
minidress dress matched the South Beach aesthetic. White
leather couches. Glow-in-the-dark artwork of palm trees.
A fog machine in a corner of the room lay beneath a black
towel, exhaling lazy plumes of smoke like a lover recover-
ing from sex. Princess had only been able to sneak me into
Parliament a handful of times since Pride. I'd mostly hid
behind her or kept to the courtyard, worried I'd get kicked
out. At Pulse, for the first time, I didn't fear being told I
didn't belong. I took a seat on the couch as if it were my living room, breathed deeply. Princess let me have a moment,
then yanked me up.

"Girl, this is the VIP section." She nodded toward the
bartender glaring at us.

We headed to the bathroom for some last-minute

touch-ups. I spat on my palms and flattened her flyaway hairs, blotted her oily skin with a toilet-seat liner, held her purse as she reapplied lip gloss. She unrolled the sleeves of my denim shirt and had me wash the X's off my hands that security had drawn to identify me as under twenty-one. "Keep them low," she said.

We split up. Princess left to mingle, and I went to the bar. Just like at Pride, older men swarmed me. They patted their laps, invited me to sit. I didn't want to embarrass Princess or have her think I couldn't stand on my own, so I played along, let them buy me shot after shot. Within minutes the loud techno music faded into a faint murmur in my ears, and I could barely feel their hands grabbing my bulge. I told myself they weren't in control, that *I* was scamming *them*, making them open their wallets. Who cared what kids from school said about me? I might have been disgusting to some boring teenagers who were probably home jerking off into their socks, but here I made grown men grovel.

Eventually I found myself lost among the bodies crammed together on the dance floor. Back at the bar, I could see Princess working over some dude, not paying attention to what I was doing at all. She must have decided I was fine without her, which made me feel like I could be too. I didn't need a babysitter. The room spun around me. I locked eyes with the nearest person, blinked through the flashing colors. He moved closer, asked me my name. I was eighteen. Finally free.

•

Mom set the door back in its frame, propping it in place with a nightstand, and pretended it fell on its own. I couldn't imagine what good would come from bringing up what had happened, so I pretended it did as well. Besides, when I pressed my ear to the cracked wood, the sounds outside were the same as they always were. The smoke detector chirping for a replacement battery. Mom and my stepdad in the living room watching TV. The only difference in our house was the oranges. My stepdad had started bringing home buckets of them once a week. He left peels over every surface, like happy, rotting doilies. Mom didn't say anything. At least he wasn't drinking. At least he wasn't hogging the bathroom.

"If wine comes from grapes," I said to Miguel one night after he'd picked me up in the Speed Queen, "you think you can get drunk on oranges?"

Miguel counted the quarters in the coin tray as he drove, Whitney on the stereo again.

"Do you have gas money, boo?" he asked, ignoring my question.

I popped open the glove compartment, rifling for more change under the empty travel bottles of liquor stored there.

"No," I said. "Sorry."

He sighed, staring at the road ahead. "You live so far from everything."

I turned to face him. The comment had come out of nowhere.

"Yeah," I said. "I know. I thought—"

"You thought . . ." he picked up the loose thread of my answer and dove in slowly, a needle piercing into fabric. ". . . what? That I'm rich? What do you even spend your money on? You don't pay cover. You sure don't ever have gas money. How much do you make at that pretzel place again? Couple hundred a month?"

"I guess."

"You guess? Well, *I guess* I lent you those shorts for The White Party and *I guess* you spilled a vodka cranberry on them. Look at you with a new cell phone. You got new-cell-phone money but not new-shorts money?"

I tried to open my mouth but discovered my lips were sewn shut. Did he have a point? Was I a freeloader? I thought helping him made us even, but did it actually cost him to be my friend? Why did he keep me around, then?

By the time we reached his apartment and entered his bedroom, my debt also included the free drink tickets he split with me, the makeup lessons, plus the "networking opportunities," which I assumed referred to those times I patrolled dance floors telling people there was a drag show in the other room, *and this one queen, I think her name is Princess, is supposed to be amazing.* I told him I'd give him some cash when I got my next check, but he said not to bother. It really wasn't a big deal. He was just nervous. Miguel stripped off his T-shirt and threw it into his hamper, where it landed on a hill of dirty fishnets, then plopped facedown on his bed.

Tonight he was debuting his Chanel No. 5 number, an

exact reenactment of the perfume commercial, down to the original voice-over and the black backless dress the starlet wears to walk the red carpet, meaning his back hair had to go. I mounted him.

"You sure it's not gonna hurt without shaving cream?" There were only enough coins in his car for a quarter of a tank of gas and a razor.

"It'll be smoother this way," he said, replacing the cap on a bottle of poppers and setting it on his nightstand. They were Miguel's favorite drug. One sniff from the tiny vial labeled "nail polish remover," and your body felt as if you were sinking into a cloud of silk. His muscles went limp as the vapors circulated through his bloodstream. My knees dug into his love handles.

I spat a glob of saliva on his back, then pressed the cheap razor to his butt crack and dragged it upward, against the grain. The dry blade plucked a strip of curly hairs off.

"¡Pero cálmate!" he yelped. "Hold on." He grabbed a pillow and bit into it.

"It's that bad?" I rolled my eyes. "Drama queen."

He nodded into the pillow, lifting his head up quickly to say "I hate you" before plunging it back down.

"*You're* the one who wants to be a girl," I pointed out. I wiped the razor on my jeans and mowed through another row. "Don't be mad at *me*."

Miguel rolled over, knocking me onto my back and the razor out of my hands. He straddled my body and pinned my wrists down. His lips spread into a smile as I squirmed.

"I don't want to be a *girl*," he said, bending down so our noses were touching. His dick stiffened against my belly, stabbing me. "I want to be Nicole Kidman." I pushed him off and grabbed the razor. "You play too much," I said. "Turn around. We're gonna be late."

The next morning I woke up with my head pounding, the smell of Fabuloso and fried food swimming in the air. Far off in the kitchen, Mom's dainty voice floated over Celia Cruz's velvety baritone playing on the radio. It would have been "La Vida es un Carnival." Or something slow and sweet. "Quizás, Quizás, Quizás." I checked my phone. There were three unopened texts, all from Lee.

Is that who I think it is? Aw, I know her!

Wait did you fuck?

They have aids. Be safe . . .

I scrolled up. There was a picture I'd sent him of me and Princess sitting on a bed in a Parliament House motel room. Her bra was tied around my head like Mickey Mouse ears. *Wish u were here!* a text message I couldn't remember writing said. *Florida misses u!*

The night trickled back. Princess running onstage being trailed by invisible paparazzi. Wrapping her arms around her shoulders, turning around, and pretending to make out with a handsome foreign man. The MC announcing the winner of amateur night: someone else. Afterward the two of us broke into a motel room and found a half-empty bottle of Absolut.

That's when we took the picture. We got so wasted we ripped our clothes off and chased each other along the shore of the private beach. There was still sand on the bottom of my feet.

no? I texted back, answering all of Lee's questions at once. He had to be confused.

I followed the smells to the kitchen, where Mom had a feast going. On the stove a pan of frijoles simmered. Next to it, slices of cheese were frying for tostones con queso, plantain discs waiting for their turn in the bubbling vegetable oil. Seeing all that fried food made me queasy. Mom swayed her shoulders to the music, eyes half-closed, that dreamy look she got when she cooked, as if any argument, any tension, could be buried under a full stomach.

"Get dressed," she said, waving a greasy spatula in the air like a conductor's baton. Faded burns trailed up her arms, matching the ones on mine from opening and closing the oven at work to remove pretzels every fifteen minutes. "We're going to church."

I sat down at the kitchen table. "Why?"

It's not that we never went. We were Catholic*ish*. A couple times a year, Mom took me to St. John Vianney and had me fill an empty Windex bottle with holy water, and later we sprayed it around the house while muttering a few Padre Nuestros. We weren't due for another refill.

"¿Como que why?" she said without losing the smile from her face. "Because we're going. Because it'll be nice. Hurry up. Eat."

I groaned and pressed my forehead to the tabletop, the cool glass surface momentarily soothing my hangover.

Mom chose two seats in the splash-zone pews up front. After a few minutes, the choir began to chant a pretty, light-filled song resembling whale music, and Padre Montoya wafted onstage trailed by a cloud of incense. He positioned himself behind the podium, spread his arms open, and regarded the congregation. The men picking lint from their baggy tuxes. The women in their most righteous peplum, already dabbing their eyes with crumpled-up tissues. Mom. Her head rested on my shoulder, hair reeking of the red dye she'd used to touch up her roots that morning. It embarrassed me how good it felt to have her lean on me.

Padre Montoya read from the Bible. Everyone said amen, repeated passages after him. When he raised a trembling finger to the vaulted ceiling and praised fiercely in Latin, Mom began to shake beside me. She was sobbing. So was the lady next to her. There were sniffles coming from all around the church. People blew their noses, coughed, hacked, wept. A baby wailed in an ancient Jesuit language. All that noise hammered inside my head. I couldn't think.

"Mama," I whispered.

It didn't make sense. Why wouldn't Miguel have told me? I knew the drawer where he kept his passport, what T-shirts in his closet belonged to his ex. Lee had to be confused.

"Mama, I'm going to the bathroom," I said.

I needed to go somewhere quiet, to replay every night we'd spent together, comb through all our conversations. Did I ever make an AIDS joke, or laugh at one? Had I ever made him think he couldn't trust me? What was going to happen to him? All I could remember from our one-day sex lesson in English was our teacher putting on a made-for-TV movie about a pregnant teen.

"Mama," I said one last time.

She wiped her tears with her wrists. "Hold it."

I couldn't.

I crossed my right leg over my left, pointed my toe, and shook it as femininely as possible. As *gay* as possible. Out of the corner of my eye I saw her staring at it. I was almost certain what was going through her mind. It was the same thing that had dominated my own before I'd come out. That someone would see me acting like that, at a place like this. That they would know what I was. I didn't care. If she really didn't either, she'd make me wait.

"Fine," she said. "Go."

I kissed her forehead and walked down the aisle with my head bowed. When I reached the bathroom, I kept going, past the ushers on standby with their tip buckets, and the gift shop, and the podium holding up the prayer book for sick congregants, pushing through the double front doors into the harsh bright afternoon.

•

I was on my knees, naked, between Miguel and a friend of his named Dez, the two of them sprawled out before me. The boys exhaled in tandem as I stroked their dicks, their backs arched over the tacky floral-print bed sheets I recognized from my first night at Parliament House.

I had to know, when Miguel called at twelve o'clock on a Tuesday to tell me his friend rented a motel room, that it was a booty call. There was no way I could be so naïve as to think we were really just going to hang out, dance a little. I had to be smarter than that. I was.

I looked down at their naked bodies, Miguel to my left, Dez to my right, and tried to figure out what we were doing, the handle of rum we'd drained in less than an hour fogging up my brain and helping me come up with this logic: Miguel didn't want to have sex with me. That would be ridiculous, him and me together. We were friends. Maybe this was his strange way of setting me and Dez up. It was kind of sweet, even if a heads-up would have been nice. Now that we were here, I might as well make the best of it. As long as it was just hand jobs and not *sex* sex, I guessed I didn't need to ask him about Lee's text. This was probably safe. Besides, Miguel should get to pick when to tell me. If it were true, which it wasn't, so whatever.

Dez trailed one hand up and down my chest. Did he know? How close were they? *We used to work at SeaWorld together* is all Miguel had said. He was still a lifeguard there. His smooth, tan body was rubbery like a dolphin's. Dez hooked his finger inside my cheek and pulled me toward his sunburned lips, brushing them against mine. I swore I tasted chlorine on his tongue. He probed it so far into my throat I gagged and backed away.

"God, you're hot," I gasped.

"Really?" he asked. Not only did I have to swallow his tongue; now I had to convince the dolphin I loved it.

"Yeah, really, really hot," I said. "You're killing me."

"You are!" He blushed, brushing my chest with his fingers again. I bent down and guided his dick to my mouth. It was already wet. He moaned, a violent, bone-rattling groan. Now I was killing him. That is what sex is, I thought. Murder. After a few minutes I looked up and saw Miguel staring impatiently at me. Somehow I'd forgotten all about him, had even stopped giving him a hand job, which was fine, because like I said, he didn't want me like that.

Miguel grabbed my head and pulled it toward his dick. I tucked my lips in.

"Um." I gawked at him, confused.

"Come on." He made sad eyes.

"I'm not really sure I . . . ," I said. "You're like my . . ." I kissed his stomach. I kissed his nipple. I pressed my ear to his chest and listened for something that would help me understand who I was in bed with, because this was not the person who, a week before, drove me to a house party one of the basketball players from school was throwing, just so I could see I wasn't missing anything. We'd parked outside and looked at the house across the street as if this were another game of bingo. Every now and then someone left, giving us brief glimpses through the open door of what was going on inside. Smoke swirling. A couple arguing. People jumping on the couch. "Weird," he'd said.

And what were we? Normal? His hand pushed down on my head. I groped the sheets to steady myself, clawing at a fistful of flowers. No, hooking up with my best friend, whose status I didn't even know, whose feelings about me were unclear, was not normal. And if I wasn't sure about those things, how certain could I be about anything? Were we really best friends, or had I skipped to that part too soon?

"It's too awkward," I told his belly button. "I'm sorry."

Miguel slapped his penis against my cheek. "Suck it," he pouted. "You did it for *him*."

I imagined standing on the balcony outside, looking in on the three of us in bed. I was a hole waiting to be filled. A donut gleaming under a display case. Drunk.

"Yeah, do me again," said Dez, seizing a clump of my hair and pulling me back to him. I closed my lips gratefully around his dick. He began to die again. It felt good to kill someone, a stranger who didn't matter to me, whereas with Miguel, the thought of lifting my head and saying no one more time made *me* want to die. My vision blurred as tears mixed with my spit. I focused on the blow job. The bed creaked, and then I heard the sound of pants zipping and the room door slamming shut.

I took Dez's penis out of my mouth. "Where are you going?" I screamed out. Miguel's silhouette lurked behind the closed curtains, pacing back and forth on the balcony.

"Hurry up," he said. "You have school tomorrow."

Without waiting for a response, his shadow walked out of the window frame.

The Speed Queen was silent on the ride home. I rolled down the passenger window to air out the smell of cum on my clothes and pressed play on the stereo.

"Million Dollar Bill" started up. I sang quietly, hoping we could act like nothing had happened. Wishing I'd just given him head. He'd done so much for me. Been like a mother. Showed me things my real one couldn't. Lee was full of shit. He'd nicknamed me Choopy Choopy before he even knew who I was, and now Miguel hated me.

He clicked the stereo off, turned to me, and said, "I have to tell you something."

"Yeah?" I said, watching the mosquitos pile up on his windshield for what felt like hours, though it couldn't have been more than a few seconds.

"I have HIV," he said.

I dropped my eyes to my palms.

"Do you know what people do when I tell them?" he asked.

I kept staring at my palms, not sure where or how to begin. "That."

"Okay," I whispered, while inside I searched for the perfect thing to say: I'm sorry. I love you. Fuck those people. Fuck me for being exactly like them.

But the words were stuck in my throat.

I'd never talked to another person that sincerely, never

had a man talk to me that way either. Men in my family patted each other on the shoulder, poured each other drinks when they were sad. Any other type of affection was territory I wasn't prepared to navigate. Even with Miguel, the thought of being completely open felt impossible. Telling him I loved him went against my instincts. If I did that to any other boy, they would have kicked my ass. But he wasn't any boy. I knew that. I knew that if there was a time to speak, it was now.

I opened my mouth, ready to try. But by then I was standing alone on my driveway, his taillights vanishing down the block.

The first night Miguel didn't text me, I sat on my bed turning my phone in my hands, angry at him for pushing himself on me, and at me for misinterpreting what we were, for not saying anything better than "okay." I considered messaging him but decided it'd be best to give him a break and let him take charge of reaching out, because I would inevitably fuck things up more.

The second night, I did my homework on the kitchen table. It was bizarre filling out my worksheets on a horizontal surface instead of pressed against a car window. Easier, though every couple of minutes I looked out through the kitchen window desperate for a beam to cut across the lawn. *Come out, come out,* he'd text, and I'd run out and jump into his car.

Not on the third night, or even that week, but eventually, I made my way over to the couch. Mom didn't acknowledge the strangeness of my hanging around the house more. I suppose she always thought I was in my bedroom.

"Are you hungry?" was all she asked, and I said, "Not really," so she made two kinds of empanadas.

We watched more interesting lives play out on-screen: María Hernández can't live with her secret any longer, but she must, but she can't, but there's half a season left, so she will.

Online pictures of Princess with another boy began to pop up on my timeline. I was jealous at first, especially about how fast I'd been replaced, the space I'd inhabited filled up as quickly as an empty spot on a dance floor. But in retrospect that also opened space in my own life. Whatever we had was over. Now there was room for a new thing to begin.

Mom and I went to Home Depot and bought a new hinge to keep my door from tipping over. Her roots grew out again. I graduated high school without buying a yearbook. I told myself these years didn't count. I'd be better off forgetting them.

One afternoon Mom took me out to lunch. Our waiter was a man old enough to be my father, gray hairs peeking through his sideburns. Maybe we'd flirted at Pulse or Parliament House before, because he placed his hand on my shoulder and called me baby.

After he left with our order, Mom leaned in and whispered, "He's cute for you."

I knew she was kidding, that this wasn't about me and him being a good match; it was her indirect way of telling me she was ready to have conversations about my being gay. Regardless of her intentions, the silence that followed was so unbearable I had to lower my head. The audacity of her attempt to gloss over the past, to do what I'd tried with Miguel: skip to the part where we were best friends. I was in denial still, but of course everything had changed when she crashed through my bedroom door, no matter what lies we told ourselves. Without realizing it I'd put up a stronger door in my mind, blocking her from accessing any part of my life she might disapprove of. We never got around to buying a new doorknob, just slid the old thing back in place so there wouldn't be a hole there. She learned to knock. When I was ready, I'd let her in.

I saw Princess around at clubs a handful of times. First, we hugged. Then the hugs turned into waving from across the room. Then smiling politely if we caught each other's eyes. There was never a big falling out. No unnecessary drama. It was as if we both recognized we'd gotten all we could from each other, and there wouldn't be any more.

I missed Miguel most on nights I felt suffocated at home. I could have called him. He might have come. But it wouldn't have been the same. So instead I took myself outside, lay in the front yard, and stared up at space like it was a vast movie screen.

I read once that in the thousands of years it takes their light to reach Earth, many of the stars we see scattered across the sky have already burned out. Turning our eyes to them, then, is like traveling back in time to when something gorgeous still existed. That's how I remembered Miguel, those nights in the yard and less and less as time passed. A beautiful and fading trick of the eye. All those flashes in the dark. It's hard to believe there was a time when I didn't know who he was. It's so obvious now. He was the most famous woman in the world.

A Room of My Own

Hector lost his on South Beach when we were kids. He'd been lying belly-down on the shore, trying to catch one of the little bugs that live in shallow holes beneath the sand's surface, bracing themselves for when the next wave will roll in and tear the roofs off their homes. Deep in concentration, my brother didn't notice the tide swelling in the distance, growing taller, stronger, finally giving birth to a wave that staggered toward him like a drunk man at a bar. Before he could understand what was happening, the wave crashed in, and in one sloppy motion it scooped up his body, yanked down his basketball shorts, and dragged his exposed penis a foot across the rough sand. Hector lay there a minute, too stunned by the sudden pain in his crotch to move. Then he pulled himself together and ran up to where I was digging a moat with Big Gulp cups.

"Are you bleeding?" I asked. I heard that happened your first time.

"No shit." He grinned, cocking one of his waxed wannabe reggaetonero eyebrows. With those two words, something bigger than a dumb moat now separated us.

As I grew older, my straight girlfriends confirmed that losing your virginity was almost exactly like what happened to Hector. "One moment, you're just, sort of, lying there," they whispered in the back of Spanish class, in line at the cafeteria, in mall dressing rooms, when I was thirteen, fifteen, eighteen, "and the next there's some blood and you feel, I don't know, changed."

"Changed how?" I asked. I imagined it'd be like the first sip of coffee, everything before it a groggy blur. After, well—

"It's hard to describe," was their collective response. "You'll see."

By college, I'd been with enough men to know it wasn't as simple as they made it seem, not for me anyway. There was Lee in the movie theater, Miguel and Dez at Parliament House. There was Alejandro, a boy from drama club. We had "sex," I guess, though I don't think I can call bending him over a bathroom sink at a public park and poking my penis in the general vicinity of his butthole until my legs cramped from standing on tiptoe a textbook example. There was Anthony, in his car. Darnell, leaning against a tree. Sergio, at night beside a quiet swamp, the two of us swatting away mosquitos. I didn't think much of these hookups, partly because they didn't seem totally real to me. For starters, these men were my friends, as opposed to *boy*friends. I viewed what we did as similar to girls kissing at sleepovers.

We were just practicing. But more than that, these episodes didn't align with the vision I had of losing my virginity, with what had happened to Hector and the women I knew. There was always some crucial ingredient missing. It was rarely lying down. I never bled. Nothing in me felt changed after. I didn't even orgasm.

So though I technically wasn't a virgin, I still regarded myself as one. My hookups were too casual, too hurried, too quickly shoved away never to be acknowledged again to count. Often they had nothing to do with attraction—hungry for love, we latched onto whoever was available as the closest substitute. The rare times we did bring up what we'd done, it was through a passing glance, or a slight smirk. My friends and I had inside jokes, not sex.

Sex with weight. Sex with meaning. Sex like straight people had that served as plot points in movies, redefined relationships, inspired characters to gaze wistfully at large bodies of water ruminating . . . about . . . *stuff.* There were people who hated me for who I liked to have sex with. If it was such a big deal, shouldn't something big happen when I had it? Something so good it justified people wishing I were dead?

The problem was location. Of course sex in a car couldn't transform me. Naturally all sex next to a swamp made me was itchy and paranoid. But it's not like I could have it at home, in my bedroom with the cracked door Mom had knocked down senior year. No matter how much she tried to make amends for that afternoon—trying to joke with me about

boyfriends, blasting the *Ellen* show at any opportunity—I
still worried inviting someone over might tip her tolerance
beyond the breaking point. Eventually we settled into a tacit
arrangement that gave us both peace. She stopped asking if
I was seeing anyone, and I didn't bring anyone over for her
to see.

Instead I lied. I like doing it outdoors, I told my friends.
In bathrooms. The park.

I didn't think I had a choice. Moving out was a totally
foreign concept in my family. In Nicaragua it wasn't uncom-
mon to see thirty-plus-year-old men living with their parents, sleeping in the same childhood beds they used to wet.
Though Hector and I were raised in The United States, it
was always understood that it would be the same for us here.
There were only two excuses to leave home: for marriage or
your education. The first didn't account for my being gay.
Hector used the second as soon as he graduated high school
and was accepted into a college in Miami. Even then, he
moved into an uncle's apartment, where he shared a room
with him and a cousin. The three of them split a bunk bed
and a leaky air mattress on the floor. The few times I stayed
over, I had to get up in the middle of the night to refill it. It
was obvious they didn't have room for another body. When
it was my turn to graduate, I only applied to the University
of Central Florida, because it was close enough to commute
to from home.

This is good enough, I insisted to myself, crawling into
bed alone after my pathetic hookups. Like those bugs on

South Beach, I adapted to living in constant terror of being exposed, burying my sex and at the same time knowing
I couldn't keep it hidden forever. Sooner or later a change
would have to come. Most nights I closed my eyes and sort
of just lay there. Fell asleep waiting for something big to
crash into my life, so that maybe then it could finally begin.

Sophomore year of college, I got impatient. One day I
pounced on Mom the moment she got home from work,
when I knew she'd be tired and easiest to persuade. Pegasus
Landing, an off-campus dorm for UCF students, was host-
ing an open house, I told her. Let's go. It'll be fun. Every
so often the two of us went on drives through the suburbs,
admiring the white picket fences, the crown molding, cracking up because our house only had mold. This would be like
that, I explained, except we'd actually get to peek inside this
time. I didn't have to convince her much. I'm almost certain
now she only got behind the wheel of her pickup truck because she didn't seriously believe I was planning to move out.
After all, where would I get the money?

What I didn't tell her was that I already had it. Six thousand dollars. Five grand from saving every penny of my Auntie Anne's Pretzels paychecks, and another thousand dollars
from selling my car after I quit. If I capped my expenses at
a thousand a month including rent, that gave me six months
to find another job within walking distance. I didn't need a
wave, just Mom's signature on my guarantor form.

After the forty-five-minute drive to the dorm, we parked in a spot in front of the leasing building. Mom examined her reflection in the driver's seat mirror, pressing an index finger to her chin and turning her face left and right. She was still in her Starbucks uniform, a black polo paired with a gray cardigan. She dabbed concealer over her dark circles, then pulled off the band holding her ponytail, unleashing her mane of greasy copper-colored hair.

"On the website," I said, trying to sound casual as she powdered her face, "I read there's this contract students need to have someone sign in case they can't pay rent for some reason . . ."

That someone, I let my silence say, is you.

Mom flipped the mirror back up. I could see the thoughts slowly weaving together in her mind like pieces in a game of Jenga. So this wasn't just for fun. I'd done research. And the last bit threatening to make the whole tower collapse:

"A contract?" she asked. Panic simmered just below the surface of her voice. This wasn't only my future I was playing with, but hers too.

"I swear you won't have to pay anything," I assured her. "Let's just go in and see. We're already here."

I stepped out of the car and didn't turn around until I crossed the front door, which was flanked by two inflatable balloon men. Inside the leasing building a party seemed to be either just about to start or winding down, given that there was no one around but me—until Mom walked in and narrowed her eyes at the still-sealed plastic box of Publix sugar cookies sitting on the reception desk.

"Where did you bring me?" she asked.

A moment later a blond woman emerged from an office. She shook my hand with the same crazed enthusiasm as the men who wrestled alligators at Gatorland. "Welcome to Knight's Circle!" she said. "I'm Jean."

I freed myself from her grip. "I'm sorry. Isn't this Pegasus Landing?" I asked.

"Yes." Jean shooed Mom and me over to a table with a miniature carnival wheel on it. "And no. Same ownership. Different everything. We're renovating. Brand-new name to go with the brand-new look." Her snappy way of talking reminded me of a bus-stop ad.

I didn't question the logic of an apartment complex changing their name simply because the units were getting new carpets. My attention was absorbed by the carnival wheel. Rainbow-themed and lit up like the one from *Wheel of Fortune*, it was divvied up into twelve slices. Each one listed a prize, ranging from Beats headphones to two hundred dollars off rent every month.

"See?" I pointed the discount out to Mom. "It might even be cheaper than it says on the website."

"You'll get a spin after signing your lease," Jean said, petting the wheel like it was her favorite toy, and if she liked us enough maybe she'd let us play with it. "First, I'm guessing you want a tour?"

She led the way toward one of the newly renovated buildings, her heels sinking into the neatly trimmed lawn as she marched ahead of us. Arm in arm, Mom and I scoped out the complex. She tried to hide it by putting on her sunglasses, but I could tell she was impressed. In the distance students lay out on beach towels next to a glimmering pool. Behind them, palm trees leaned into the sky like paint brushes against a clear white canvas. Other students streamed out of a building I'd read online was a lounge where free movie nights were held, laughing and holding their bellies as if they'd just stepped out of a brochure. This wasn't a dorm. It was a luxury resort, and the two of us were the hired help. Mom buttoned her cardigan up to her neck, covering the green Starbucks siren embroidered on her chest. I kissed her cheek. Her skin reeked of sweat and coffee. There was something both of us must have been thinking but didn't dare say: this place was so much nicer than our house. After our water pipes burst earlier that year, we didn't even have a shower. For months we'd been bathing outside with the garden hose, crouched low behind open umbrellas so our neighbors wouldn't catch us.

"It'll probably suck," I whispered to her, suddenly overwhelmed with guilt. When she got ready for work in the middle of the night, it was too cold and dark out to shower. Sometimes she did when she got home, a precious moment I'd robbed her of by dragging her on this tour. With the savings I'd kept hidden, I could have paid for a plumber, or a real outhouse, given Mom a week off work. A cousin in Nicaragua needed braces. An aunt recently lost her job. It was selfish to want a room of my own. Why did I need one? Because I was horny? Change? What the hell was I talking about? This was stupid and cruel, for both of us. Moving out was not an option.

Jean guided us into the living room of a model apartment and made a sweeping motion over the gleaming hardwood floors. New, she told us. New microwaves. New fridges. New stoves. New carpets in the *bedrooms*.

She smiled, her teeth bleached to Vanna White perfection. "That's what you really want to see, isn't it?"

I nodded, though part of me wondered if it would be smarter not to. If I didn't remember what I couldn't have, then I wouldn't miss it.

There were two bedrooms in the unit. Jean opened their doors and stood us between them so we could see clearly into both. One had a blue accent wall. The other pink. The light streaming in from the windows inside made them glow like portals into better lives. I chose door number two.

It was larger than I expected, bigger than Mom's and mine put together. A queen-sized bed was tucked into a corner. Next to it were a dresser and a hardwood desk, the latter decorated with generic girly items: a bowl of sea shells, an old issue of *Cosmopolitan* magazine, gum. I couldn't help picturing myself having sex on top of it, like in a movie, swiping that crap to the floor and daring a man to *take me right here*. Everywhere brimmed with potential. Sex on the carpet. In the closet. Pushed up against the pink accent wall. *Be as loud as you want*, I could hear a future version of myself saying.

"The room comes with the dresser and desk," Jean said,

interrupting my fantasies, "plus the bed. Though you'll have to provide your own sheets, of course."

Thank God, I thought, chuckling politely. These were yellow with adorable purple polka dots and reeked of the plastic bag they came in. No one fucked on sheets like that. They handwrote letters to their grandmothers and attached copies of their report cards. Five dollars for every A.

"So?" I asked Mom.

"It's cute," she admitted.

I sighed. It would have been.

"Time to leave the nest, huh?" Jean caught the two of us off guard. We turned to her and put on the fake smiles we used when strangers spoke Spanish to us. "One more thing," she added, opening a door I'd thought led to the closet. "Every room comes with its own bathroom."

I could have fallen to my knees.

"Please," I begged Mom, forgetting everything about being a good person. My cousin, my aunt, they probably would have joined my mother in battering down my door. Why did my savings have to be communal when love in our family wasn't? A vision of myself taking a hot shower pushed them out of my mind. No more hoping the wind wouldn't blow the umbrella away. No more watching the ground through one soapy eye to avoid stepping on a frog or slipping on algae. "You said yourself it's cute," I pleaded. "Please. Please. Please."

I knew she hated that I was doing this in front of a woman who looked like Jean. I hated that I was too, but I was desperate and didn't know what else to do. This trick had worked before, when I came out to her at Saks. It embarrassed her to make scenes around white people. Mom's eyes darted from Jean to me, her cheeks flushed. Jean smiled awkwardly.

"Okay," Mom said at last. "Okay. Fine. Gasta tu dinero pues."

I wanted to tell her to repeat herself in English. Tell me that wanting this little thing for myself was a waste of money so everyone could understand. But it was more important that I impress Jean. If Mom and I argued about rent in front of her, she might not think either of us could afford the apartment.

I threw my arms around my mother and smothered her with kisses, squealing, "Thank you! Thank you! Thank you!"

Back in the leasing office, we stood in front of the carnival wheel. Mom finally looked excited. Like me, she loved game shows, playing the lotto, anything that didn't take account of your current circumstances and guaranteed you'd be taken care of if you had enough faith. Hence my TV production major: any job with *TV* in the title had to lead to money. I placed my hand on one of the spokes. This slice of the wheel promised two hundred dollars off monthly rent, which would have lowered it from $650 to actually-affordable-to-a-recently-unemployed-twenty-year-old. I calculated how much force I'd have to exert for the wheel to make an exact 360-degree spin but quickly decided this wasn't a matter of science, it was destiny. I closed my eyes and pushed, listening to the spoke flicker through all my possible futures—one where I could have *disposable income*, one where I could afford a new laptop. When the wheel came to a halt, I opened them and followed the arrow pointing to my prize: a twenty-five-dollar iTunes gift card. Mom tried not to laugh.

"Can I go again?" I asked.

"No," Jean said.

It took me a week to discover that another man lived in the apartment. The day I moved in, I'd knocked on the door to the second bedroom to introduce myself, and no one answered. Maybe the roommate management had told me about was at work or school, I thought. Three days later, he still hadn't appeared, so I tested the doorknob. It didn't budge. No noises came out of there. No light was visible under the frame. I connected those facts to the empty living room, fridge, and cupboards and assumed a bureaucratic error had been made and I had the whole place to myself. I wasn't about to complain, especially if it meant I could walk around naked belting Mariah Carey.

His name was Benjamin, he told me the night he came out of the bedroom, dark indents under his eyes, skin the sallow color of Red Bull. I was in the kitchen, wearing nothing but white briefs. I scrambled to cover myself with a cereal box and made an excuse about having just come out of the shower, even though my hair was dry.

He knew I was moving in, he said, voice scratchy and new, as if these were the first words he'd spoken in a while.

But he lost track of time while working on his latest video-game design project ("Oh, that's my major," he said) and forgot to say hi. His bad. From that I gleaned this wasn't going to be a sitcom living situation where we'd hang out at the campus coffee shop and talk about who we were dating. That was fine. I wasn't here to make friends.

I went through the requisite stats. I'm majoring in TV production. Twenty years old. Nicaraguan and Puerto Rican, but I was born in Miami and grew up in Orlando.

Then I changed the subject to what was really on my mind. What was up with our apartment? It bore almost no resemblance to the model Jean showed me. The lawn surrounding it was yellow, and where there were patches in the grass, weeds had been planted and cropped close to the ground, like hair plugs. Inside our unit the floors were scratched up, the living room walls haphazardly painted with broad white stripes that went in all directions, as if they'd been colored in by a drunk child. My bedroom window had blue electrical-tape X's crisscrossing the glass to protect it from the last hurricane that hit Central Florida—almost a year earlier.

"I've been here six months," Benjamin said. "They keep saying they're going to move me to one of the renovated buildings, but at this rate those will be ready after I graduate. That's why they changed the name to Knight's Crossing. People kept complaining online. You didn't read the reviews?"

No, but I did see on the Pegasus Landing website that they were screening the new Harry Potter movie in the movie lounge, which turned out to be a room with a flat-screen and a handful of folding chairs. Our building was so far back into the complex you had to take a special shuttle that came by twice an hour to even get to it, or to school.

I still thought life there was an upgrade from my mother's house, so I kept my mouth shut, though this explained why the apartment was empty. Benjamin was waiting to get transferred. Even so, I didn't understand how he could live so bare-bones. I'd only moved in a few days earlier, and already I had three times the amount of stuff he did. There was $350 left in my monthly budget after rent. I ran through nearly half of it at the Walmart next door, where I bought a vanity mirror for my bathroom, shower curtains, a cork board, plus all the little things I'd assumed, incorrectly, I'd be able to split with my roommate: dishes and silverware, pots and pans. Mom stole bags of coffee from work as a housewarming gift. She also offered me twenty dollars for groceries, but I turned it down—to have savings *and* take her money would have been evil. I rode the shuttle to the leasing office every morning to grab handfuls of candies from the receptionist desk and used them to supplement my diet of dollar bagels at the campus Barnes & Noble. I was so broke that when I ran the numbers on my budget, I couldn't help but clap my hands and laugh, but at least I owned a toaster. Benjamin had nothing.

"The last guy who had your room used to have weird people over all the time," he said all of a sudden. "He was a . . . I mean, I'm not . . . You don't smoke weed, right?" It looked like the question pained him.

I clutched the cereal box closer. "No," I answered.

Sure, my old coworkers at Auntie Anne's had given me a cigarette box full of joints as a going-away present, and, okay, I'd been smoking weed since I was thirteen, and, all right, it was the middle of the day and I was in my tighty-whities, but no, I wasn't a drug dealer; no, I wouldn't be bringing my weird friends over; no, he didn't need to be scared of me.

"Cool," he said, "because, yeah, the last guy . . . but . . . cool."

After that night we barely saw each other again. I supposed he was busy designing another video game. If someone were to stand between our bedrooms and see through our closed doors, to the left, they would have found Benjamin slouched over his computer, energy-drink cans stacking up on his desk. On the right, me jamming a towel under my doorframe, walking around with a joint in my hand and a smile spreading across my face, running my fingers across my bed, along my wall, digging my toes into the carpet, all of it mine. Stoned, I played a game.

First I imagined the smoke was from a fire.

Then the rules: Your house is burning. You have time to save one thing.

A month in, I still hadn't had sex on my bed. Or against the wall. Or on my desk. But I wasn't worried. Soon I was bound to bump into someone on my way to class. My books would fall to the floor. We'd both get down on our knees to gather them up. I'd say, *I'm so sorry,* and he'd say, *It's nothing.* We'd look deeply into each other's eyes, and out of my mouth would emerge the six most beautiful words in the world. *Wanna come back to my place?*

Until then I distracted myself looking for work. I bought black trousers, a black sweater, loafers, and extra-hold styling gel at Walmart to slick my hair back and took the bus to a nearby shopping plaza. I applied everywhere a manager would see me. Between my class-time restrictions and the fact that my only experience was twisting pretzels, none of them seemed interested. "Come back when you have more availability," one told me. During an interview, another asked what I would do if a customer wanted a blouse and we didn't have her size.

"Is it cotton?" I asked.

"Why?" she asked back.

"Well, if it's cotton, I'd tell her to get the next size up," I said, "and put it in the drier so it shrinks."

"Oh no no no, honey." She sneered, as if I'd recommended that, instead of buying a new blouse, the customer take a look at her wardrobe and put something old back into rotation. "You suggest another item in a similar color or style."

Clearly she'd never wanted something so bad you'd do anything to make it fit.

Despite my still-absent source of income, I refused to admit I couldn't afford my room. When I had to dip into next month's thousand dollars to pay my phone bill, lowering my food-and-household-items budget to a little over thirty dollars a week, I remembered something a classmate from high school said when she'd gotten accepted into her dream college. I'd asked her how she was going to pay to move across the state, on top of tuition and boarding. Everyone I knew was going to UCF or community college, not because we didn't have the grades to go to more elite schools but because, at forty bucks an application, merely applying cost a small fortune.

"I never thought I'd get in," she said matter-of-factly. "And I got in. Money isn't going to stop me." I thought she was delusional then, but I understood her now. I never thought I'd get to move out, and I had. Destiny would sort the rest out. I just had to put myself in its path.

At a bulletin board on campus one day, I saw a flier for a student-run free food pantry. It wasn't a long-term solution to the growing emptiness in my stomach, but I was too hungry to think any further than dinner. I disguised myself in sunglasses and a hat when I went, distressed by how soon into supposed adulthood I was already failing.

There was a girl behind the counter I recognized as a fellow TV production student. Brandy was a former beauty queen with aspirations of being a news anchor. She wore a full face of makeup and two-piece suits to our 9:00 a.m. seminars. I imagined her house, probably one of those with crown molding, was full of actual crowns. She looked up from her shiny MacBook and said hello as snappily as Jean had months earlier. I panicked. Instead of telling her I wanted food, I asked if the pantry needed volunteers. "You have no idea," she said, and hired me on the spot.

Aside from food, the pantry stocked household items like toothpaste and deodorant, baby necessities, and school supplies, as well as anything else frat houses and local churches donated. The job didn't pay, but it would look great on my résumé, Brandy told me during my tour of the small building. All I had to do was sit at the front desk and check each student's ID, offer them a bag, and make sure they only took up to five pounds per day by weighing their items on a scale.

A large portion of the pantry regulars, I soon discovered, were students who lived on campus who didn't want to take a bus to the local grocery store. They strolled in and snatched bags of chips from the shelves like it was their kitchen. This infuriated me. Whereas I was too ashamed to ask if I could have anything, fearing what Brandy would think—that I was, for the second time in my life, the scholarship kid (I was), that all people of color were needy (I did need)—they took casually, unchained by the guilt that what they were doing would reflect on anyone but themselves. Others really did depend on the pantry for food. They spent half an hour deliberating between what they wanted and what weighed the least. When I was eventually trusted to be left unsupervised, I let them have as much as they could fill their bags with, and I started bringing home food too, items I told myself no one else would miss: dented cans of green beans, oily jars of peanut butter that had separated long ago. I smoked my gifted weed to make the expired food taste better.

Then the stash ran out. No longer able to stomach what I took from the pantry, I lost fifteen pounds in two months. My tighty-whities got baggy. Worried about what Mom would think if she saw how skinny I'd become or how barren the apartment was, I claimed I was too busy for her to come over, promising she could visit as soon as I was more settled. In class, I grew more and more anxious about my dwindling savings as the group projects we began working on grew costlier. I bribed friends to star in my short films with lunch, was the first to offer five dollars for gas when group projects took us off campus so my classmates wouldn't suspect anything. Still, I couldn't keep up. Without my own expensive editing software, I could only practice at the computer lab for a few hours a day. All of my classmates seemed to own professional-grade video cameras and drones, gifts from family members who worked at Disney or Universal Studios. Their short films looked like blockbusters. I saved face by calling mine experimental and made up for the bad quality by spending more time on my scripts, the only thing I got compliments on during class screenings. Competing with them, there was no way I'd get the internships I needed to make a career in TV.

It dawned on me around this time that I would never have money. Why would I get lucky when the only person in my family who didn't live paycheck to paycheck was my engineer uncle in Nicaragua? Even if I did somehow beat out my competition and secure a high-salary job in television production, my paychecks would go toward supporting my relatives, just as my uncle's income was redistributed among us. In a way, accepting that my circumstances would not be dramatically impacted by my future income was freeing, because if I surrendered to the inevitability that wealth would always be out of reach, then I could stop wasting time pursuing it and focus on what made me most immediately happy. The alternative—outmaneuvering racism and classism and homophobia only to end up sitting miserably at an office doing more of the same—hardly seemed like the better option. Buoyed by my classmates' compliments, I tacked on a creative writing major, not discouraged by the people who warned me there were no jobs and no financial stability in the field. I already didn't have either. At least writing was free.

Every now and then, cute guys would come into the pantry and flirt, though in retrospect they probably just wanted me to break the five-pound rule for them, which I gladly would have. They smiled sheepishly at me from behind rows of cans of diced tomatoes and lingered longer than other clients. "What should I eat tonight?" one of them asked me once, handing me his groceries to weigh. His tank top clung to his chest, glued there by butterflies of sweat.

I blushed and told him what he could have if he only asked: "Whatever you want, man."

These brief flashes of romance assured me I was getting closer to sex, the whole point of moving out. As the weeks passed, I fed on the hope that one of them would find the nerve to ask me on a date.

At home one night, the vanity mirror in my bathroom fell, shattering on the floor and scattering shards of glass across the tile. A few large chunks of mirror were still stuck to the frame, and because it wasn't in my budget to buy a new one, I simply put it back up. My reflection was broken up into jagged slices, but there was enough of me to get a rough idea of what I looked like. The glass on the floor I swept behind the toilet and left there. I don't know why. Maybe I liked thinking that if this were Mom's house, I would have had to clean up right away—while the glass was still on the ground, the shards reminded me that here, I had control over my own life. Maybe I wanted to be punished for betraying my family by being greedy with my money, and I felt I deserved it every time I cut my foot. Maybe I was lazy.

A week later the bathroom light went out. I replaced it with a novelty red lightbulb someone donated to the pantry. The floor became a minefield, and showering felt like a scene from a horror movie, but the new lighting made the stains in the sink less noticeable, and I couldn't justify spending four dollars that could go toward food, so I kept it.

With only the pantry job, I had endless free time. I got back into my high school habit of drinking coffee until I became delirious, only now, instead of projecting myself into rom-coms, I wrote them. There wasn't much else to do without a car or a job or money. Blacked out on coffee, I told myself I was a starving artist.

Part of me must have known I was going to have to give up the apartment soon. By then there were enough savings left for just two months, and even if someone hired me, with minimum wage hovering at below eight dollars an hour, I would have had to work full-time to keep my room. Possibly drop out of school if the job couldn't accommodate my class schedule. The reality of returning home was too heartbreaking for me to fully process without a glimmer of hope to hold on to, so I monkey-barred onto my next escape plan, what would sustain me when I had to go back to living with Mom and my stepdad. Writing. That would make me rich. Then I could be a good person, save everyone, and leave, permanently.

Once I accepted that my days in my room were numbered, I felt the same relief as when I gave up on TV production. If I didn't have to worry about applying for jobs anymore—Auntie Anne's would surely take me back—then for the remainder of my time at Knight's Crossing, I could stop trying to pass as straight. While applying for jobs, especially if the manager who spoke to me was a man, fearing my voice was too high-pitched, I'd always lower it to a grunt. At Mom's, my stepdad used to pace outside the bathroom door groaning if I spent too much time doing skin care. He'd side-eyed me whenever I left to hang out with friends in outfits he deemed girly, whether because my jeans were too snug or because I had too many accessories on. The problem was that I was *too*. Obvious. Much. So I made myself less. Threw out the necklaces, the rings. Let my acne flare.

I would have resented Mom for not standing up for me, but I was beginning to learn there was only so much we could sacrifice for each other without giving ourselves up entirely. She already worked herself ragged, picking up extra shifts when my stepdad was in between jobs, doing all the cooking and cleaning, not once asking for rent. What about *her* life? Her dreams of opening a Nicaraguan restaurant and driving a shiny black Jaguar convertible? Defending her son might push her husband away, and then what would she have? An effeminate boy she couldn't bring around the family? A house that would have been worth more on fire? I'd allowed it to fall into disrepair so I could save money. That's what I chose when I played my game.

Me.

Now, in my room at Knight's Crossing, I painted my nails, uninhibited by the prospect of having to shake a hiring manager's hand or shove them into my pockets following a disapproving look from my stepdad. In my bathroom, wearing a long T-shirt, with a towel wrapped around my head in imitation of a beehive hairstyle, I spent hours pretending I was working the red-light district of some faraway city. My purse was a Walmart bag. My arched feet, on tiptoes to avoid glass, were in heels. Presented with so much liberty and with little time to adjust, I was nouveau queer, like those people who win the lottery, immediately buy beach-front mansions in Miami, and fill them with bearskin rugs and Fabergé eggs, only to go bankrupt within months. I got to choose how I walked, how I dressed, who I was, so in my eagerness I chose to prance, wear every color, and be proud, all too aware that soon this good life would run out.

What surprised me the most was how quickly the guilt I felt for putting myself before my relatives faded. What replaced it was something similar to what I expected to feel but didn't when I told Mom I was gay in high school. Happiness. It hadn't been enough to come out of the closet if what awaited me on other side was just a larger room for me to hide in. No, I'd needed room to grow up.

At school I became someone else, shedding the old me in favor of a new one who wore butterfly clips in his hair and cutoff shorts so tiny the boxers underneath showed. I danced to class. Hummed in the hallways. I was not a hit. As I backslid to being "too" again, the boys at the pantry lingered less. It was obvious that I could experiment with my appearance or I could have sex, but I couldn't do both. It'd been four months and I hadn't been on a single date. No one had bumped into me. In fact, the queerer I looked, the more distance students kept from me.

One afternoon I wrote an ad on Craigslist looking to rent out my room for the remainder of my lease. While I was on the site, I wandered over to the Personals section to read the latest dating ads, something that had become a hobby of mine. I thought of the regular posters as characters in a novel, like the woman who copied and pasted this one twice a week: *Single Momma Seeking Kindness and Companionship. No Assholes.* Though we were both alone, it comforted me to know she was out there. We weren't alone in what we wanted. I often wondered whether she'd had any luck, if she'd gotten any bites. On weeks she didn't post I cheered her absence, imagining she'd found someone. When inevitably she returned, I mourned the love lost as if it were my own, while simultaneously celebrating on behalf of her kids, who wouldn't have to deal with an intruder in their home.

This afternoon, I brewed a pot of coffee and, before I knew what I was doing, hit "publish" on my own ad. Heat rose to my ears as I stared at a listing someone who seemed nothing like me had written. *Bored College Student Looking for Fun*, it said, followed by words that weren't nearly as beautiful, highlighted against my lurid screen: *Wanna come to my place?*

I met Ricardo by the pool, just in case he wasn't the five-foot-nine uncut Venezuelan medical student he claimed to be in his response. The first thing he did when he saw me was laugh. I'd wiped the nail polish off and put on a tank top and basketball shorts before leaving my apartment, figuring he wouldn't be into that other version of me. Now I lowered my head, suspecting he could see through my stupid act, or that he simply thought I was ugly.

"Don't be shy," he said, pushing up on my chin with his index finger. "You're really cute. It's just, this is weird, but my girlfriend lives here. It's so . . . convenient."

I felt my chest expand with relief, and then I felt like the worst person in the world. "Your girlfriend?"

"Don't worry," he said. "She lives closer to the front of the complex."

Suddenly I couldn't focus on anything but his sweatpants and sandals. An outfit you wear to take a short walk. What did he tell her, that he was going out for cigarettes?

"Does she know?" I asked, already knowing the answer. Still, I was supposed to ask, right? Good people ask. Maybe I wasn't a good person, but I had to be better than those people who pretend their actions won't hurt anyone. Shame was close enough to empathy. I heard his answer, grabbed his hand, and pulled him to my apartment, full of it.

"Do you have a roommate?" he whispered once we were inside. He glanced around the empty living room. A lawn chair I'd found in the dumpster faced a blank wall. If he thought anything of it, he kept his opinion to himself.

"Yeah," I said. It was dark under Benjamin's door, but I knew he was in there like always, leaning toward his computer screen like a low-light plant. "He's chill. Come on."

In my room, I asked him his last name, his favorite book. Details I needed to convince myself he wasn't a stranger I met on a website where people sold used car parts. As free as I thought I was, I still had a lot of discomfort with the idea of casual sex. But if this was *making love*, that was different, just like it was different when it was with friends.

He sat on the edge of my desk and picked up a framed picture of me and Mom dressed as a clown and a cowboy on Halloween when I was a kid, then laid it facedown and removed a Black & Mild cigar from his pocket, tearing the wrapper open with his teeth.

"Is it cool if I smoke in here?" he asked, already lighting up.

I looked everywhere for an ashtray, almost offering him the picture frame before I found an empty green-bean can in my trashcan. When I set it next to him, he pulled me between his legs and palmed my ass with one hand while the other held the Black. I tried not to think about the ash that was building up on its tip breaking off and burning a hole in the carpet. About my security deposit. About his girlfriend, who I didn't want to hurt but didn't plan on letting stop me either.

I rested my forehead against his and told myself we would only hook up once, that I was helping him get this out of his system before he returned to her, the person he really cared about. I was doing them a service. How could she be upset with me, when she had everything and I had what? Her scraps, and only long enough for him to walk to the store and back. Our noses touching, I set my sight on his bronze skin, the little mole in the corner of his lips. Looking down into his shirt, I could see ripples of muscle slicing across his body.

Ricardo let a trail of smoke slither out of his mouth in a way I suppose he meant to be sexy. The fumes stung my eyes. A tear rolled down my cheek and landed on his shoulder. I licked it off before he could notice. He moaned. It tasted like everything I deserved.

"Be as loud as you want," I told him.

"Huh?" he asked, leaning back to see my face.

"Forget it," I said. "I didn't say anything."

He put out the cigar in the can and slid a finger under the band of my underwear. "So, what are you looking for tonight?"

"I don't know," I said. "You."

He squeezed my ass, smirking. "Should we shower first?"

The thought that he would use my bathroom hadn't occurred to me until then. "It's a little messy in there," I said, "but okay."

I slid my tank top off and threw it on the bed. His sweatpants dropped to his ankles. He stepped out of them as I pulled down my basketball shorts. We stood facing each other naked, our dicks hardening between us. Plumes of smoke trailed out of the green-bean can and swam in the air. I couldn't take it anymore. I embraced him. He hugged me back. We held each other up, like the foundation of a house of cards, daring someone to come try to knock us down.

I left the lights off and guided him quickly into the shower so I wouldn't have to explain the mirror or the glass. We lathered our bodies with shampoo. Our hands caressed whatever parts they happened to find in the pitch-black room. A thigh. An arm. Eventually we both stood beneath the showerhead, water falling onto our heads, enrobing us as we kissed.

"I want you," said Ricardo.

"Me too," I said.

"No." He took his lips off mine. "I want you right here."

"Oh. Okay." I turned around and braced myself against a wall. He kissed his way down my spine until he found the part he needed, then spread me open.

"Do you have lube?" he asked.

I looked over my shoulder at the shadow behind me. "No. Sorry."

"It's fine," his disembodied voice said. "We can use water."

I turned back around. "Go slow," I said to the wall. "I've never bottomed before."

I took a deep breath. His fingers squeezed into the meat of my waist. I felt something poke into me, the tip of his cock maybe, and it was just barely unpleasant; then suddenly a sharp fire ripped through me. I gasped but couldn't breathe. My knees buckled. I flailed my hands in a panic, trying to push him off, pull it out, to hold on as my vision curled like a burning photograph, closing in at the edges. Finally I surrendered to weightlessness as the world dropped from beneath my feet. The last thing I remember is hitting something hard and cold.

Little by little I came back. My soaked skin was wrapped corpse-like in a thin plastic sheet. Everything was red. My legs and the side of my stomach stung. Cuts. For a moment I thought I was in a morgue. I tore what I realized was the shower curtain off me, blinked up at the red lightbulb. A man knelt over me, wiping shards of glass off my skin. Ricardo. His voice faded up in my ear.

"Fuck fuck fuck," he was saying. "Are you okay?"

"What happened?" I sat up and brushed what was either water or blood off my arms. My head throbbed where my skull had hit the floor, a lump rising there. I buried my face between my knees.

"You passed out." He rubbed my thigh. "You don't remember? You grabbed the shower curtain when you fell. I think you broke your mirror too."

My memory slowly seeped back. We were in the shower, about to start. One moment, I was waiting, my heart thrumming with anticipation, and the next, the next . . . "It's hard to describe," my girlfriends had told me. But I could. It was like someone jammed a roll of sandpaper up my asshole. It fucking sucked. *This* was what I'd screwed my mom over for?

"I don't . . . I can't . . . ," I started to say, then gave up, humiliated.

Before I could understand what was happening, Ricardo scooped me into his arms, stumbling as he lifted me up. He kicked open the bathroom door and carried me into my room, gently placing me on the bed. I lay still as he propped a pillow beneath my head and draped a blanket over me. He sat down and took my temperature with his palm, worry etched across his face.

He was a good boyfriend, I thought. She was lucky.

"Can I get you anything?" he asked.

I shook my head. I didn't want to talk. I didn't want to do anything for the next twelve months. Just sink into the mattress, stain the sheets, become a permanent fixture of the room.

"Broken mirror," he said and frowned. "You know what that means."

I searched his face for a clue. "No, what?"

"Seven years bad sex." He laughed at his own joke.

I rolled over. My butt was too sore for this.

"Sorry," he said, squeezing my shoulder.

I rolled back.

"It's not your fault."

He stood up and looked down at me pitifully.

"I should probably head out," he said.

"Yeah."

"You all right?"

I shrugged.

"I'll text you." He bent over and kissed me on the cheek. For a moment I imagined what we would be like together if he stayed, whether we would be happy, or rich, or okay, then I returned to reality with the sound of my bedroom door opening and slamming shut. His footsteps echoed across the empty living room. I closed my eyes, lay there for a long, long time. If I didn't dwell on what I couldn't have, I wouldn't miss it.

Boy's Club

From the edge of the pool, the water looked a perverse picture-book blue. Moments earlier I'd arrived and caught a couple having sex in the deep end. The men jumped out at the sight of me, the word *creep* flashing in their eyes, as my scrawny arms gripped my towel over my belly button. I must have looked like a boy in this men's club, someone to skirt around. All that was left of them now was the trail of drops that fell off their waxed asses as they stormed away and the glimmer of a condom wrapper winking on the water's surface.

I dipped my toe in and flinched. Club Orlando's website claimed the pool would be heated, but the staff must have decided to leave the thermostat off, figuring no one would be in the mood for a swim on this chilly Florida night. Locals take out their thickest hoodies as soon as the weather drops below eighty degrees. Most don't think, Time to go

to the sex club. When I decided to come, I don't know that
I was thinking at all. I rubbed the goosebumps off my arms
while I waited for my body to acclimate to the cold, trying
to forget the naked man who had sent me running out to
the pool in the first place. The image of him lying facedown
on a massage bed was too fresh to easily wash away. How
he'd squirmed when he heard my footsteps enter his private
room. The bluntness of his desire: Come closer. Fuck me.

Club O wasn't a joke for him. He probably didn't have to
make fun of bathhouses with his friends before rallying the
nerve to drive over. I'd told one I was coming for the free
HBO. To another I said I was on a missionary trip. The last
friend rolled his eyes before I even finished telling him I was
writing an "investigative report." I was going to break this
case wide open.

The water frowned up at me, bored by my childish games.

I'm not really here, I wanted tell it, as if that wasn't obvious. I'm just, I don't know, *looking*. This wasn't any different
from Parliament House bingo. The pool's surface could pass
for a sheet of glass. I just wanted to peek into other people's
lives. Compare them to mine.

While I stood there frozen in place, the old slurs rushed
to my head. Maricón. Faggot. My mother's hard face when
I answered her that, yes, I was one. Every time I said to a
classmate in high school that I was gay but that I was different. Different how?

I'm not like other gay guys: if you get too close, you'll see
that I'm made entirely out of matchsticks meticulously glued

together. I'm not like other gay guys: instead of eating, I soak my body in a tub of chicken broth overnight.

No.

I'm not like other gay guys: I can remember the first and last name of every man I've slept with. I'm not emotional. You don't have to worry about me tricking or getting AIDS or going to a nasty bathhouse. I am not chicken.

I could have left by now, driven home. But I couldn't imagine one more night of falling asleep with my legs wrapped around a pillow. I didn't want to be that kind of gay guy either. My fingers loosened their tight grip on my towel. It fell into a pile by my feet like an old snakeskin. Suddenly I was naked, and then I was underwater, watching the world through a sterile blue fog.

In 2013, a standard room at Club Orlando cost twenty dollars plus tax on a weekday, twenty-eight dollars plus tax on a weekend. I shouldn't have been surprised about the tax—a bathhouse is a business, after all—but still, I couldn't help wonder how many sidewalks and public schools were funded by two men giving each other blow jobs in a hot tub. In an effort to draw in a younger crowd, Club O had discounts for those twenty-three and under. I was twenty-one at the time, so I got in at the comparably bargain price of thirteen dollars, the cost of a locker, no room.

I went at 2:00 a.m. on a Tuesday. Even at that hour, there was a line to the front counter. A man in front of me checked his phone, presumably reading work emails flagged Very Important, and tugged impatiently at his T-shirt. When it was my turn, the jaded employee on duty gave me a weary look and asked for my license, which he would keep for the duration of my stay. He pushed over a liability waiver. It said that if I should acquire any sexually transmitted diseases while on property, I would not sue. I handed it back with a first-day-of-school smile. In exchange, he gave me a pair of keys on a bracelet.

Because I'll be naked later, I thought. Of course. No pockets. Oh God.

The receptionist eyed me up and down, probably thinking I was overdressed in blue jeans and a plaid shirt, buttoned all the way to my neck. My one chance to wear flip-flops to the club, and I picked Converse.

"You know the rules?" he asked.

I lied and said yes.

Maybe by habit, he nodded at a metallic plaque on a wall behind him and turned back to the portable television on his desk.

"You have six hours," he said, eyes glued to his screen. "Enjoy."

I skimmed the plaque: always use protection, no alcohol allowed on premises, blah blah blah, rimming inadvisable. Nothing I hadn't already learned from my mother.

I stood there half expecting something else, someone to come out and explain what to do next. When no one did, I drifted over to the reception area. Two empty couches and a small coffee table faced a flat-screen where a sci-fi movie about giants at war was playing. Past that I could see the locker room, consisting of a small smattering of benches and wall-to-wall lockers. I made my way inside, wandering through several rows before I found mine, forty-three, jammed between dozens of others.

The key wouldn't turn in the lock. An amused-looking man a few lockers down noticed me in trouble. He swung a gym bag over his shoulder and clapped a rough hand over the back of my neck.

"Need some help?" he asked, smiling.

Jesus, I thought. I hadn't taken my clothes off and already I was in a bad porn. *Horny Dad Seduces Helpless Latin Twink*. I shrugged his hand off and watched him tinker with the key, knock the locker door once here and once there. It popped right open. He stared at me with a self-satisfied grin, waiting, I supposed, for me to drop to my knees and unzip his jeans. Something about him reminded me of all the older men who bought me drinks as a teenager in exchange for a feel. Yeah, no. I could buy my own drinks now. I crossed my arms and braced myself for whatever cheesy line he was going to throw at me.

"Well, be safe!" he said, then strolled away unbothered.

My arms deflated to my sides.

Good! Perfect! You're not here for sex anyway, I repeated to myself, a little bummed that it wasn't even on the table. The age discount had led me to believe I'd be a novelty among the mature crowd at Club O, but I must not have been that appealing, that special. I undressed and folded my clothes into a neat pile, placing them far back in my locker. From a nearby rack, I grabbed a complimentary towel and wrapped the scratchy fabric around my torso. This was an assignment, a case. I was a private investigator. My starch-white towel was my trench coat. I was exploring alien territory to see if maybe I could be make a life here. No one could push me to the margins if I drove there willingly and paid to get in.

I gave myself a moment to accept the reality of what I was doing. I was alone, practically nude in public, not breaking any laws. The words *This is so weird* settled in my mind for the first of many times as my locker door clicked back into place, my underwear stashed safely inside.

I followed the purr of vending machines to what Club O's website referred to as the "cafeteria," though the space was so small it managed to be lit by a single lightbulb. I scanned the room, taking in two dingy vending machines, a fold-out table, and a microwave splattered with dull yellow stains. Food was not allowed into the premises, I remembered from the plaque with the rules, so if someone were to develop an appetite at any point during their six-hour stay, they would have to purchase something from one of the machines. I walked over to them. The first was completely empty. The second featured one row of Juicy Fruit gum, the rest of the sleeves stocked with Cup O' Noodles. I thought of someone devouring a cup of freeze-dried meat chunks floating in brown, lukewarm water, then scurrying over to the sauna for a casual round of anal sex, and felt my soul slip out of my body.

Club O was open twenty-four hours, which was why I was able to be there so late. I assumed this also meant all cleaning and restocking had to be done during operating hours. Considering these facts, and the paltry cafeteria selection, only one person could be responsible: the vending machine deliveryman.

It's his first day on the job, and Club O is his first stop. His coworkers conveniently forget to warn him about what kind of place this is. Club Orlando? he thinks before entering, taking note of the palm trees and trim garden out front. The property is massive, completely at home with the CVS across the street and the Petland adjacent to it, just another stop on your way home from work. Must be some sort of country club, he decides. He takes a similar route to mine, past the disenchanted front deskman and the reception area and into the cafeteria. He's on his knees shoving packs of Sun Chips into the machine when a naked dude walks in, his skin still pink from the steam room. The deliveryman hears his footsteps and turns around, only to discover, inches from his eyes, a shriveled penis like a spring roll over a slimy bed of dumplings. Instinctively, he jumps to his feet—*What the fuck!*—makes a run for the company truck—*What the fuck!*—presses play on his *Metallica Greatest Hits* CD—*I am not a fucking fag!*—and speeds home, where he will have sex with his wife for a manly ten minutes before washing the gay off him by pouring a warm Budweiser directly onto his head. He will not be amused when his coworkers laugh at him the next morning. He will never go back.

That was my theory, anyway. There had to be a reason for why this was all we had to choose from. Cup O' Noodles and gum. Gay bars and sex clubs. Or maybe I just wanted to imagine someone doing what I was desperate to do: get far away from here.

Whatever the truth was, Club O was stuck serving gas station food. Probably it was stocked by the front deskman between episodes of whatever he watched at 2:00 a.m. on a weeknight in 2013: *Seinfeld* re-reruns? A ShamWow! infomercial?

The faint din of EDM on the speaker system beckoned me out of the cafeteria. Tuesday seemed like the best night to come to the bathhouse. The website promoted the club's quaint Sunday poolside cookouts, its Thursday Popcorn Movie Night. I needed to make sure I could handle an average visit before tackling whatever one of the themed nights might entail. After all, this place advertised itself as a gym. Who knew what Popcorn Movie Night *really* meant?

The music led me into a dark, narrow hallway. I could hear men grunting behind the thin walls on either side of me. The hallway grew darker the deeper in I went, until eventually I was lost inside a pitch-black maze, taking small, careful steps as I blindly groped through the void ahead of me. Dimly lit chambers punctuated the walls, some wide open and others curtained off. Moans slipped under the fabric. Skin slapping against skin. My heart pounded in my ears. I burst into the first quiet room I came across, searching for an exit.

There I found a man cuffed facedown to a leather

massage-bed. The wisps of hair winding down his lower back stood on end. I moved closer, unsure whether it'd be rude to tap his shoulder and ask for directions, drawn forward by a mix of desire and curiosity. He lay still, a mass of quiet, eager white flesh. I looked around for a sheet of paper he'd maybe scribbled instructions on before asking someone to help tie him down. Of course, there was none. It was obvious what he wanted: a man to climb on top. To take him. His reason for being at a bathhouse was so sincere that I was suddenly uneasy with my own jumbled motives. When I told myself I was not like other gay men, I meant him. I was not loose. I didn't just let things happen. He was the image I was afraid would flash before people's eyes when they discovered I was gay.

And yet here we were in the same room.

And yet, if I wasn't at Club O to have sex, then what was I here for?

For kicks? To have a laugh? The thought of that sickened me. At least he was honest. At least he knew what he liked. As if it had a mind of its own, my hand reached toward him. I pulled it back, gripped my towel closer, and tiptoed into the hall again, closing the curtain behind me. Minutes later I located a real exit and staggered out of the maze.

The door deposited me in the large courtyard with a pool. I froze. Two men treaded water in the deep end. They were in their own perfect world, oblivious to the boy twenty feet away from them and the bubblegum Katy Perry song pouring out of the sound system. It was hard to tell whose hands were holding what, whether they were sighing or panting. I saw lips, heard giggles, felt jealousy rising in my chest. Do you love each other? I wanted to ask. When did you stop being scared of all this? How? Please, show me. One of them noticed me ogling. He leaned into the other man's ear. The two quickly unglued themselves and shot me looks that made it clear I was intruding. Behind me was the building I ran out of. In front, the pool. There was nowhere to go. I stared at my feet as the men scrambled out, only daring to look up when the sound of their angry footsteps receded and the door to the maze slammed shut. You can leave too, I thought. Right now. Go home, chicken.

I stayed underwater longer than I should have, curling into a ball and letting gravity drag me to the rough floor. Spotlights lining the bottom of the pool gave birth to bright, ethereal beams pushing their way to the surface above. Motes of dust floated in their centers like humans sucked helplessly up by UFOs. Every cell in my body burned, pleading for air. All my instincts—all anyone—ever told me was that if I wanted to survive, I had to deny myself what I ached for. The touch of another man. Bad places like this.

My chest burned. My fingernails dug into my thighs. I waited through the fire and, when my eyesight began to blur and the distance I could see around me closed in, I waited through that too. I don't know how I knew I was ready, I just knew, either in the marrow of my bones or from my brain warning me that I could keep hiding down there and drown or I could be gay. Enough already. I thrashed my way up and out and gasped for air, inhaling the Martian atmosphere ravenously. In my delirium, what surprised me most was that it didn't harm me at all—my head didn't explode like I'd learned in high school would happen if an astronaut were to take off their helmet. I took in more air, breathing greedily, funneling it into my famished lungs until they were satisfied and buzzing. It was totally safe. Not just safe. Good. Everything I'd been taught about surviving was wrong. I wasn't surviving before. I was existing.

I sat at the lip of the pool, heady from this new knowledge. There was a heaviness inside of me. You are here, the heaviness said. *You* are here. You *are* here. You are *here*.

So, then, be here, I thought, shaking off the water, wrapping myself in my towel, and heading back inside in the same direction as the couple I'd scared off earlier.

As I made my way through the club, I began to recognize the men I saw, the same way you recognize tourists when you are also one. An older man with saggy breasts. A muscle daddy running his finger along a twink's rosy cheek. All of them with a look in their eyes. Relief. To have discovered people who spoke the same language.

I found another hallway, this one lined with dim light-bulbs. Small, round cutouts at about waist-height pierced the walls. Eyes followed me through the glory holes. I speed-walked until I arrived at a door. Plumes of steam snaked around my feet when I opened it. A sauna. Inside I fell onto the nearest seat on a low wooden bench, beside a silhouette. I felt more eyes on me in the hazy room and prepared to run again. Then an anticlimax: from a shadow came forth an arm, extended in peace. It introduced itself as Carlos.

"Hey," he said.

"Um, hi," I said back, confused by the small talk. I only had my towel on, and he was very naked. His sweaty balls were crumpled between his legs like paper bags left out in the rain. I couldn't exactly ask, So how about the weather?

"It's nice, actually," Carlos answered when I did. "I'm from Chicago. It's freezing there."

He was on vacation with his sister and brother-in-law. He heard about Club O from a friend of a friend and decided to check it out. Much like me, he was looking, though when he said it, it had a different connotation. I was looking, and he was *looking*. I barraged him with questions, trying to buy myself some time: What do you do? How old are you? Have you ever done this sort of thing? He managed a grocery store. Twenty-eight. No.

I told him about a television show I'd recently gotten into.

"So there's this girl and she's a private detective at her high school. Well, she's not really a private detective. Her dad is. But she works for him. Like, unofficially. She goes around solving crimes and mysteries and stuff."

He listened politely, indulging the twenty-one-year-old trying to solve his own mystery. At the opposite end of the sauna a pair of lips parted in a wide, toothy smile, like the Cheshire Cat's. His name was Byron, he told us, emerging from a cloud of steam, frizzy locs roping down his back. He used to be a boxer. I pictured him in a ring, hopping foot to foot while an oiled-up girl in a skimpy bikini held up a Round One sign. I wondered what made him retire, why he came here and for what.

Byron slid over next to me and placed his hand on my thigh. His fingers crept down to my crotch. Carlos moved in after him and grabbed the corner of my towel. The getting-to-know-each-other portion of the night, I guessed, was over. I locked eyes with Byron, hoping Carlos would take the hint that I wasn't interested. A hand caressed my bulge. I was too nervous to find out whose it was. My heartbeat accelerated. You're not my friends, I thought, not in an ill way, but truthfully. You guys just want to fuck me.

"I have to go," I blurted out in a panic. "It's really hot in here."

I gathered myself and slipped out of the sauna, the door hissing as it slid shut. Across from me were open gang showers. I wandered toward them, keeping an eye over my shoulder to make sure the door stayed closed. It did. My anxiety melted away, replaced with awe over what had just happened. Two men looked at me and assumed I was at Club O for sex. Maybe I wasn't quite ready for that, but it excited me to know I could play the part. This was all acting.

I stepped under the closest showerhead, dropped my towel, and turned the nozzle. As water drummed against my skin in cool, leisurely beads, I closed my eyes, stuck my face up to the stream, and laughed, swinging my hair around like a model in a shampoo commercial. The thought of Carlos and Byron coming out and realizing how wrong they were was the funniest thing in the world. Me? An object of desire? Me? Here for a casual hookup? I pretended to massage conditioner into my scalp, cackling deep down in my belly. Girl, what is happening!

The sound of footsteps approached. I opened my eyes, not thinking about the showerhead pointed at my head. A gush of water drilled into my face and slapped one of my contact lenses out of place. The plastic held on to my eyelid, then rolled down my cheek. I trapped it with my palm, rushed out from beneath the shower, and leaned against the nearest wall.

Right then a tall, muscular man walked into the showers. I crumpled down to the tile floor, cradling the contact on my fingertip as he lathered his toned arms and legs with soap, so impossibly beautiful, whereas I was so impossibly naked on the ground at a sex club, laughing. Suds coursed down his body and drained into a vent by my feet. Again, it hit me how much of a fraud I was in comparison to everyone else. I was a child pretending to be a reporter, pretending to be a model, pretending that this was a funny story, anything so I wouldn't have to be who I really was.

I picked myself up and fled to the bathroom, where I maneuvered my contact back on in front of the sink mirror. I blinked until my vision gradually came into focus. After the pool, sauna, and showers, I'd never been this clean in my life. I stared at my reflection, brushed off all those other costumes until I saw just one thing, what I recognized in everyone else: a foreigner who had traveled a long way to be here.

The voice from the pool whispered in my ear again. Then be here.

I returned to the showers, collected my towel, and strolled back into the sauna. Carlos was gone, but Byron hadn't moved. He sat smiling the same big smile as before. *Hey.* I slid onto the bench and wiped the steam collecting on my forehead with my arm.

"What do you want to do to me?" he asked, not wasting a second. He rubbed his fingertips up and down his thick thigh.

I crossed my legs, not sure how to answer. I wanted to be like him, the kind of gay guy who could ask a question like that. Or like all the other people I'd come across. The man in the massage bed, the two lovers in the pool. But for some annoying reason, all I could imagine myself doing with him was going on a date, telling him about my favorite show, sharing a Cup o' Noodles in the Chill Lounge.

I didn't understand why I wanted those things back then, but I do now. As much as I wished I could shed all my shame in one night, I was still too afraid of Club O, of what it would mean for me to feel at home at a place designed for quick sex. It was easier to tell myself I wanted what wasn't being offered there, because as long as I pined for something else, what was actually within my grasp couldn't frighten me.

Byron waited for an answer.

"I'm sorry," I finally said. That I wasn't better at this. For wasting his time. Being a tease. Before I could finish apologizing, he leaned in, quieted my lips with his. I reached out to push him off but discovered that instead of fighting, my hands were pulling him closer. I spread my legs apart, guided his fingers down, granted him permission to touch me, not the person I hoped I was but the parts of me that couldn't lie. He held my hard dick in his hands; I buried my nose into his strong chest. For a second, in that hot dark room, we inhaled each other's breaths.

"I'm sorry," I said one last time, hating myself, and left.

On my way out of Club O, I approached the front desk again. It was near dawn now, and the man behind the counter was slouched low in his seat, his eyes glazed over. I traded in my bracelet for my license and shoved it into the back pocket of my jeans. The fabric of my damp shirt clung to my chest. Every contour of my body felt exposed, bared for any stranger to inspect. The man yawned and turned back to his rerun. He was unimpressed. I was not special. Not a one-of-a-kind gay guy. He had seen this one before.

Everything Is Sexy!

Savoy, where the bartender kept a shotgun on the shelf above the register "just in case," wasn't the kind of gay bar where anyone went to seriously *fall in love*, right? So we weren't bad people, I told my best friend Arturo, hoping that saying so would be enough to make it true, the same way that it's okay to say something mean as long as you follow it with, "Was that mean?" even if you don't take it back. We weren't bad people, because this wasn't a joke: our competition to seduce the same guy. This wasn't like those movies where the popular boy asks out the nerdy girl as a prank. I really did think the man we'd picked was beautiful, nursing a drink alone at the bar, one ear pierced like George Michael. And in the unlikely event that we did *fall in love* five feet from a loaded weapon, great. We'd have a shotgun-wedding theme. The Ke$ha track playing on the jukebox could be, like, our song.

But first I needed to get Arturo to focus and stop asking

me about a conversation that happened twenty-four hours earlier. The one in which my boyfriend Eric dumped me.

"He said that? 'You're too femme'?" Arturo yelled across the low metal table between us. He placed his hands over mine, covering the fingernails I'd painted black in mourning. In the dark corner where we were huddled together, it must have looked like he was reading my fortune. "What does that even mean?"

"Come on." I pried my hands out from beneath his. "Let's do this before he leaves."

Arturo leaned back and crossed his arms, the sleeves of his navy-blue hoodie stretched tight over his biceps. "I just need to know if I gotta go fight someone."

"Relax," I said. "Okay, no, he was too nice to say, 'You're too femme,' but trust me, that's what he meant."

Eric thought my clothes were too . . . curated. My interests were too . . . indoorsy. "You don't act like you anymore" is the exact phrasing he used to end things. *I* wasn't *me*. I'd been so dazed that I drove straight to Dunkin' Donuts and picked at a cruller for an hour, wondering, Well then, who are you? until I decided that most immediately I didn't want to be a twenty-three-year-old having an existential crisis at a Dunkin' Donuts and staggered back out.

"Whatever. I'm over it."

"Good," said Arturo. "That guy sucked anyway."

"That guy," I repeated. That was who he was now. I supposed that was who I was to him too, if he was talking about me with a friend. That guy. That guy who played him.

Listen, I never told Eric I was masculine. I just didn't say I *wasn't*. He assumed I would be, because Latino men, you know, that's our default. I knew it the second he messaged me *Hey papi* on Grindr, like that would endear him to me. I knew he thought I'd be like all the tan boys on TV. His very own dangerous-yet-privately-charming gangbanger. The hot-blooded, half-naked gardener invited in by the bored housewife for a glass of iced tea. Right away I should have corrected him, should have written back that I'm not anyone's papi, most definitely not some random white dude's. I could have used it as a teachable moment, told him those stereotypes that cast Latin men as savage and sex crazed have been historically used to suggest we're all rapists and Bad Hombres who need to be tamed.

But, girl, he had abs. He had *that V thing*. Plus I was a little tipsy and Grindr isn't school.

So I responded, *Hey baby*, and kept my eye rolls to myself when he peppered our flirtations with his junior high Spanish. If he only thought of me as his macho Latino fantasy, I figured I had a free pass to return the favor and use him too. Is that mean?

It wasn't till the following morning that I took it one step too far. We were having coffee in his bed. My lips were still swollen.

"It's my day off," Eric said. He brushed his knuckles against my inner thigh. "Do you want to keep hanging out? I know a spot around here where we can go hiking."

I'd already done so many things with him outside my

comfort zone. Had a casual hookup. Been the top. What difference would it make to keep going?

"Yeah, hiking sounds fun," I answered with a fake-deep voice.

A few days later he invited me over again. We drank Bud Lights in his backyard and practiced with his archery set, which I was both impressed and mortified by. All our dates were like that. Enough good in them to make the embarrassing parts fade into the background. We held hands while watching football, made out all night to Fall Out Boy. Eventually, at his coworker's wedding, when he introduced me to the bride as his boyfriend, a surprise to both her and me, it was too late to reveal myself. Fuck it, I thought. Be Papi. Don't you deserve this?

Over time I gradually drizzled in the real me, like a mom disguising broccoli in a child's smoothie, hoping Eric wouldn't notice that I was more femme than he'd signed up for. One day I ordered a cocktail instead of a beer. The next week I bleached my hair. Four months in, he tasted the broccoli. You should have seen his face when I said I didn't really identify as any gender. And he was white *before*.

I wasn't me anymore. Ha! Being yourself is for straight women experimenting with bangs, not sissies.

Arturo must have known this. When we first met in middle school, we were both girly-boys. I used to admire his skinny jeans and studded leather belt. He helped me practice doing splits. Years later when we got close again in college after going to separate high schools, I discovered my friend kickboxed twice a week for fun, whereas I spent most nights lip-syncing alone to Mariah Carey in my room. In private, I wondered if he'd gone the smarter route. Some facial hair and a few spritzes of woodsy cologne and everywhere we went dudes swarmed around him like pesky mosquitos. If he could change, if it was as simple as it looked, then why shouldn't I? The problem of my femininity wasn't an unsolvable one. It wasn't that I was ugly. Eric proved that. It was that who I *was* was ugly.

"You ready?" I asked Arturo. Over at the bar, George Michael sat watching a Madonna video playing on a monitor on the wall. I'd already seen his profile on Grindr when we stepped into Savoy. *No fats no femmes*, it read. I wanted to see if a person like him could look at me like I wasn't repulsive—to know if I could fool someone again, or if Eric had been a fluke.

"Take this seriously," I said into my drink. "And don't let me win just because you feel bad."

"I don't feel bad," Arturo said. "You're better without that loser."

"I loved him!"

Liked him. Liked how he laid his eyes on me that first morning, when I still tasted good.

"Shut up. No you didn't. He was boring."

"I'm boring."

"I love you," he said. "You know that?"

"Stop. I'm fine. If I wasn't, would I be about to hit on someone else?" I smiled with all my teeth. "And don't go easy on me! I'll know."

"All right." Arturo unzipped his hoodie and tied it around his waist, freeing his toned biceps. "But don't get your feelings hurt."

I tucked my bleached blond curls behind my ears and volunteered to go first. Here's what you don't know, I told myself as I marched across the grimy linoleum floor toward George: pop music, how to hem a pair of pants, the pros and cons of various ChapSticks. Here's how you talk: In rough. Clipped. Sentences.

"Hola," I said, sliding into the stool next to him. His hairy chest was tinted red from the neon lights advertising tonight's five-dollar drink special: a beer and a shot.

"Sup," he said.

"So, what are you drinking?"

He held out a beer between his thumb and index finger and gave it a quick shake, his eyes still glued to the monitor.

I had another idea.

"Do you know where the bathroom is?" I asked.

"Sorry?"

"The bathroom? Where . . ."—I narrowed my eyes—"is it?"

This doesn't sound like a very good line, I know. In fact, it sounds like the *worst* line. But trust me when I say that it works. It goes like this:

You approach a stranger at a bar. Make flirty small talk, a comment about his hair or what he's drinking. Oh, a beer? I've never had that! Is it good? Can I try? If he plays along, ask for directions to the bathroom, all the while conveying, through a subtle, suggestive squint, that you do not actually have to use it, but that he should, if he's interested, follow you there. Wink, wink. Twice, men understood me completely. We rushed to the bathroom, locked the door, and made out until a crowd formed and a leader was elected to bang on the door. The line *works*.

George Michael shrugged. "I've never been here."

"No worries," I assured him. "We can find it together."

"I'm good. Aren't you the one who needs it?"

I winked.

He stared.

I winked again, in case he'd missed the first one.

"I just really have to use the bathroom." I bit my bottom lip like the girls in his music videos. "If you know what I mean."

He cringed.

"Never mind," I said, then dragged myself back to the table, where Arturo tried not to laugh.

"What happened?" he asked.

"This is messed up." I contemplated the maraschino cherry at the bottom of my glass. "We're, like, using a person? To validate ourselves? And we're okay with that?"

"Gosh." Arturo swiveled in his seat to face our poor victim. "You are so, so right." He left to take his turn.

I watched his muscular back bend over the bar, his fingers steal a pen next to the register. He scribbled something on a napkin and dropped it in front of George, then whispered into his ear. They laughed. Two shots appeared in front of them. They licked the salt from their wrists. I picked at my manicure. Black flakes fell from my fingernails and disappeared onto the floor.

That guy. I was that guy. It wasn't long ago we were slow-dancing at his coworker's wedding. I'd pressed my head against Eric's chest, the two of us woozy on champagne.

"So I'm your boyfriend?" I asked.

"I wasn't sure how to introduce you," he said. "But yes. If you want to be."

I pulled him in closer, holding him tightly.

A new track firing up on the jukebox brought me back to Savoy. George and Arturo were still talking by the bar. Falling in love. Five feet from a loaded weapon. They looked good together. Great. They could have a shotgun-wedding theme. This would be, like, their song.

Even though he did nothing wrong, Arturo felt guilty that I'd lost our stupid game. In the days that followed, he tried to reassure me I was beautiful. Via text. Call. And when I avoided those, Grindr, where he messaged me at noon on Saturday: *Damn, baby boy, bring that fine ass over here.* And 2:00 p.m.: *I just want a taste!* 10:00 p.m.: *He was psycho anyway. You should have seen the shit he texted me.* 10:03: *You wanna go out? Let's try again.* Worse than getting turned down was the idea that Arturo would think of me as his needy, insecure friend who required constant cheering up. Besides, his insistence only made me more doubtful. If I really was beautiful, it would be obvious, not something he needed to prove to me.

I blamed Polylust, the burlesque troupe he'd recently joined, for his new lovey-dovey, body-positive attitude. He hadn't told me much about them other than their name and that they were taking a "radical" and "alternative" approach to stripping. Polylust's first show was just around the corner, and they were, Arturo said, calling it "Everything Is Sexy!"

Because he was my friend, I held my tongue, though I could think of several things that weren't sexy: Mountain Dew, phantom-limb pain, adults who are really into Disney. "Everything Is Sexy!" smelled like snake oil. Like those articles that try to rebrand stretch marks as lightning bolts. What if the skin on my ass just stretched? What if some of us aren't? Sexy?

If the thousands of hours I spent watching rom-coms as a teenager had taught me anything, it was that beauty is a limited resource, accessible at any given time to exactly four tall people with brilliant dentists. It was supposed to be that way, exclusive, otherwise it wouldn't be special, wouldn't have made me feel chosen when it messaged all five feet seven inches of me, *Hey papi*. It was precisely that rarity that drew me to Eric. He was a precious commodity, a "safe" gay, one of those who never gets clocked while walking down the street. In my Grindr profile picture, I must have looked that way too. Shirtless, with my fingernails out of frame, I was a blank slate for him to project any personality onto.

Naturally, the personality he chose is the one he wanted. Masc 4 Masc.

In the real world, however, being a blank slate wasn't as simple as taking off my shirt and snapping a flattering image. I had to be hypervigilant about keeping my voice low, not crossing my legs, not using words with too many s's. When I spent the night at his place, I washed my face with hand soap, as opposed to the half dozen potions in my skincare routine that would have given me away. By morning my forehead would be tight and greasy, but I'd be lying if I said it didn't feel good to wake up in his world. How much it thrilled me when we ran into the grocery store on a beer run and people didn't narrow their eyes at the gay couple, because they didn't see fags. What they saw were two friends.

I'm tired, I finally wrote back to Arturo.

I meant it. Too tired to go to another bar and walk up to another man and say "Hola." To sit at that same bar stool and listen to that same song, the one where I secretly hoped I was hiding enough of myself to be someone else's Latin fantasy. He could go. He earned his fun. I was good in my bedroom, lip-syncing to Mariah Carey.

The night of "Everything Is Sexy" with an exclamation point at the end, I drove to the venue known by word of mouth as The Space, a generous euphemism for what it was: an abandoned studio apartment above a pizza shop on the outskirts of downtown Orlando. I paid my five-dollar cover and found a spot in the second row of a crowd full of girls with half buzzed hairdos and boys wearing shimmery eye shadow, all of us behaving as if it were perfectly normal that we'd gathered in a room with no air-conditioning to watch strangers tear their pants off.

The performance area was a half circle of Christmas lights taped to the hardwood floor in the apartment's former living room. Next to it, a Post-it note stuck to a tin bucket read "Tip, Bitch." That was it as far as decorations. Someone unplugged the lights, plunging The Space into darkness, then plugged them in again to signal that the show was about to begin. The opening notes of Depeche Mode's "Personal Jesus" were piped into the room, and Joanie Waters, the first performer, shoved her way through the crowd until she was alone "onstage."

Though she was the mother, or founder, of the troupe, she was dressed in a schoolgirl outfit: a plaid miniskirt with a white blouse tied into a frilly bow above her belly. Topped with a ratty blond Halloween wig, she looked straight out of a John Waters set. Apparently that had been the point. Later I'd find out she borrowed her name from the cult-film director famous for casting a drag queen as his leading lady.

Beside me, a guy in a shredded band T-shirt nodded along to the moody electronic song. I tried to follow the beat, but the closest to goth I ever got was the *Buffy* theme song. I mouthed the word *watermelon* a few times, a trick I'd learned from Princess when she forgot her lyrics, and took a swig from a lukewarm bottle of Absolut that was being passed around.

Joanie prowled behind the Christmas-light divider,
making sure everyone got a moment to appreciate the fine
details: her winged liner, the shiny gloss lacquered over her
snarling, red lips. My nose clogged up with the scent of her
candy perfume.

Bypassing the hassle of teasing, she ripped her blouse
open straightaway. Her teardrop breasts hung three steps
from my eyelashes. Electrical-tape X's crisscrossed over her
nipples. Band T-Shirt nudged my elbow and whispered,
"Bro."

The blouse fell to the hardwood floor, where it met
Joanie's foot. She twisted her heel into the fabric. Two stage-
hands emerged from the crowd, their shadows melting into
hers on the wall behind them. One eased her arms into a
fringed leather jacket. The other fetched a lit pillar candle.
Through a cracked-open window, the sound of Friday-night
traffic penetrated the stuffy room. Joanie scowled like a
caged beast, sending a shiver pulsating through the audience. She was done warming up. Snatching the candle from
the stagehand, she threw herself onto the ground and held it
up to the ceiling as if it were an offering. Melted wax pooled
around the flame. There's no way, I thought, and covered my
mouth with my fingers.

She tilted it.

Molten-hot drops hit her bare breasts. The wax snailed
down her skin, hardening around her heaving stomach. My
own chest burned. A deranged smile spread across Joanie's
face. Her eyes moved over the room, seemingly taking note
of our reactions. A woman behind me examined her toes.

Another threw a crumpled dollar bill into the tip bucket. Band T-Shirt kept his elbows to himself.

Joanie hoisted her body up, the wax cracking as she moved. A slice of it weighed down the tape on one of her breasts, causing it to peel off and uncover a nipple the color of guava paste underneath. Joanie blushed. *That* was too much. She closed the leather jacket tight around herself and ran into the room next door smiling and waving goodbye, trailed by applause.

One by one, the rest of the troupe performed their numbers. "Everything Is Sexy!" was a vague enough theme that there was plenty of opportunity for interpretation. A short, chubby woman with angelic dimples, introduced as Miss Andry, rolled out a barrel labeled "toxic masculine waste" and took a bath in green goo to the *Breaking Bad* theme song. Arturo, who used the stage name Havana Gold, slashed his clothes off with a machete until he was down to a pink tutu, then performed an elegant ballet to Patsy Cline's "Crazy." I felt that way as I watched the rest of the night's performers.

Crazy and exhilarated and confused. Why were they doing this? To bare yourself to a room full of strangers was wild enough, but to be weird on top of that and call it sexy? Where did they get the balls to be so bold?

Being naked in public, one of the most googled nightmares, is said to symbolize vulnerability, a fear of being exposed. A convenient infographic on a U.K. mattress dealer's website claims nightmares about nudity represent "not being able to find yourself, uncertainty, or feeling wrongly accused."

If Polylust was the exact opposite, people who stripped down to their bedazzled jockstraps while wide awake, perhaps the symbolism could be inverted as well. These people had found themselves. They were certain of who they were. They did *that*.

Polylust rehearsals were structured with one basic teaching strategy in mind: relentless positive affirmations.

"Get ready to shake that fucking shit, motherfucker!" Miss Andry hurled at me from her seat on the floor at The Space. We were in the room where I'd first seen the troupe perform a month earlier. She took a bite from the greasy slice of pizza on her lap and wiped her mouth with her furry arm. Maya was really feeling her burlesque character. Miss Andry was the alter ego who possessed her when she performed her routines, which typically involved the humiliation of men. I was all for it, but just not right now, minutes before I was supposed to show the troupe the rough draft of the dance I'd been working on for their—our—next show, "Everything Is (Still) Sexy!" Surrounding me were Arturo, or Havana Gold; Joanie Waters, known to her college students as Miss Reid; and a violently supportive mob of half-naked strangers whose names I hadn't memorized yet, so I called them "y'all."

As in: "I'm sorry, y'all. I don't know what I'm doing. Thanks again for letting me join. Sorry. Thanks."

"Shut the fuck up!" screamed a woman with baby-doll heads dangling from her earlobes. She rested on her elbows beside Miss Andry, her frizzy black bangs matted with sweat as if she'd freshly given birth to her earrings. "You're gonna be amazing, dumbass!"

I nodded at Joanie to play my song. She shot me a thumbs-up. Prince's "Kiss" sprung out of my phone's wimpy speaker. I tucked my baggy rehearsal T-shirt into my sweatpants and jumped into position, my legs spread apart, my hands at my hips in the Wonder Woman pose I'd read was scientifically proven to make you feel powerful.

No one told me a shift would happen, that I'd go from Edgar to Johnny Deep—the stage name I'd chosen for myself—when I stepped onstage, but I assumed that was how the troupe mustered the nerve to strip: for the duration of their songs, they forgot who they really were and their alter egos took over. I bowed my head and waited for Johnny to slip in. The troupe stared at me, possibly wondering if this was part of my routine. Building suspense. Teasing. It was not. Miss Andry sucked out the last dregs of her coke.

Twenty-five seconds into "Kiss," I was supposed to be sliding off my shirt right as Prince squealed about not needing experience to turn him out. Instead I stood there trying to get my leg to stop shaking. Johnny wasn't coming. Okay. I inhaled. Okay. You be sexy, then. Just you.

I raised my right arm and flexed. My puny bicep swam

in the loose sleeve of my shirt. I gave it a little peck while discreetly calculating how mad at me Arturo would be if I sprinted across the room and dove out the window. He'd hyped me up so much to the troupe that they waived my audition. I kissed my other bicep and moved my hips stiffly to the beat. At the very least I had to finish for him.

"Hell yeah!" he yelled.

Miss Andry broke character, slapping her thigh and screaming, "Oh, daddy! Oh, *please*, daddy!"

I peeled off my shirt and flung it by my feet, then dropped to my knees and prepared to do push-ups like the male strippers I'd watched on YouTube the night before. The men who looked like me invariably dressed in leopard print or ambiguously Native American costumes, and they always finished their routines writhing on the floor like wounded animals. Despite the performances I'd seen at "Everything Is Sexy!," it didn't occur to me that I should try to do something weird or femme empowering. I was new and wanted to impress. Papi was tried and true.

"Daddy, please!" Miss Andry yelled.

I've heard professional dancers say that when they're really connecting to a song, they black out and lose themselves in the music. Doing push-ups in front of strangers, carefully, so that my nose didn't brush against the filthy hardwood floor, was not like that. I knew exactly how dumb I looked. I could see Arturo in my peripheral vision stretching his legs. Could smell the sweat pooling under my armpits. Seven push-ups in, I collapsed as Prince broke out into a guitar solo.

Miss Terri Machine (who borrowed her alias from the *Scooby-Doo* van) yelled, "Bitch, I'm wet! My pussy is literally flooding!"

I appreciated the sentiment, but I was clearly awful. It was obvious that in their desperation to democratize sexiness, the troupe was willing to cheer for anything. Even if they weren't lying, they were praising the tough-guy strippers I was impersonating, not me, and so their words only further proved that my instinct to play into those stereotypes had been correct. Arturo could get away with embracing femininity because he had the body of a G.I. Joe. For him it was unexpected, subversive. For me it would have been redundant.

"Damn, where'd you learn to do *that*?" Joanie asked.

Already sprawled out on the ground, I gave up on choreography and did the Worm, trying not to think about the last time this place had been swept.

"You're killing it!" she shouted. "I'm dead. Fucking deceased!"

As the song sputtered to an end, I pulled myself up and brushed the dirt off my stomach, then trudged to the sidelines, where I kept my head low and watched everyone else rehearse.

"Clean it up, baby!" Miss Andry yelled at Arturo as he wiped the floor with his perineum to Brooke Candy's "Opulence."

"Eat it!" Joanie begged Miss Terri Machine. In her lunch-lady-inspired strip, she dumped two cartons of cottage cheese on herself and lathered it over her body in ecstasy. "You like that cheese, you cheesy slut?"

Miss Terri Machine squeezed her breasts together. "I loooove cheese," she cooed.

Her real name was Megan. She played the piano in her church choir.

In my bedroom that night, I tried to shove rehearsal from my mind. The troupe would probably find a way to politely kick me out soon, and that was fine. Who cared if I wasn't cut out to be a stripper? Loads of people weren't, and somehow they managed to live full, satisfying lives.

From my nightstand, I grabbed a bottle of cocoa butter and squeezed a dollop onto my palm. My freshly showered skin went from gray to gold as the lotion melted into my arms under the glow of the warm overhead light. Touching myself made me feel cute by reflex, my body remembering all those times I'd prepped for a date.

What if I was? The question dipped its little toe in my mind, curious if it was okay to go in. Sexy? I closed my eyes and pictured myself onstage. Not at some shitty studio apartment. A sold-out arena. Madison Square Garden, with thousands of people hungry to watch me get naked.

I pulled up Spotify on my laptop and typed in the word *sexy*, pushing past my embarrassment as the images the word evoked flashed through my mind: piña coladas, wild stallions galloping through a meadow, those space-age condoms with multiple heat settings. The first result was Marvin Gaye's "Sexual Healing." Perfect. Corny enough that I wouldn't have to take myself too seriously. I pressed play.

Over a soft bed of snare drums, Marvin's smoky voice whispered at his baby to wake up, because he was as hot as an oven.

Eyes locked on my reflection in my vanity mirror, I superimposed a silk blouse and patent leather jeans over my towel. It didn't matter that I wasn't savage or feisty or macho or spicy, or that I lived with my mother, who was only a thin wall away. Thousands of eyes were on me, a sex MD, waiting for my healing.

I trailed my fingers down my chest and wrapped them around the edge of my towel, yanking it off as pyrotechnics exploded behind me. The crowd at Madison Square Garden lost their minds. Security had to hold them back as I spun the towel over my head and tossed it their way. A starved hand reached up. The hottest person alive—Rachel Maddow/The Rock—caught it. They sniffed the damp cloth and shuddered at the smell.

"You are the sexiest fucking thing I've ever seen!" they yelled.

I pretended to unbutton a pair of jeans and hooked my thumbs inside the belt loops.

"We would die for you!" Rachel Maddow/The Rock screamed, louder now.

I drew them down, inch by inch, until I was standing naked. A soft tingling began at the nape of my neck. It crept down my chest, past my belly button, all the way to my toes, which curled with the sudden urge for a man to shove me into bed. I threw myself facedown onto my mattress, rolling around on my cool sheets, just as Rachel Maddow/The Rock burst through my bedroom door. No, thundered in on a stallion, a fancy hot condom clenched between their teeth. "Baby," Rachel Maddow/The Rock bellowed. "I'm hot just like an oven!"

I buried my head in my pillow and laughed, feeling sexy, silly. I kept laughing, trying to hold on to that feeling, to not think, for a few more seconds, about how joyless I'd allowed my real life to become.

"You are sexy," I whispered in the shower the following morning. I cringed saying it out loud. If it was true, I was conceited. If not, sad. I said it again anyway. "You are sexy." The words echoed against the bathroom tile, smoothing out the hesitation in my voice. One of my favorite games as a kid was Bloody Mary. If you're not familiar: you lock yourself in a dark room, say "Bloody Mary" three times into a mirror, and wait for her corpse to materialize and, like, kill you or something. Though she never showed up, I was certain it wasn't because she didn't exist, but rather because I'd butchered the ritual by not lighting the correct number of candles, or maybe by pronouncing her name in the wrong language.

"You are sexy," I said one last time. Nothing happened.

Confidence didn't crawl out of the drain. But it wasn't the fault of the words. I wasn't trying hard enough.

Afterward, as I rifled through my closet for my day's clothes, a sense of daring took over me. I pushed aside the uniform of mostly jeans and plain T-shirts I'd reverted to after moving in with Mom again, and from the back I pulled out a faux-snakeskin shirt a friend had given me as a birthday gift. I'd only worn it once—to the mall. A young boy in the food court had been delighted by it. The shimmery fabric was like something you might see swimming in an aquarium. I remembered the boy wanting to touch it, his finger reaching out. His father yanked him away before he could. For a second I considered putting it back. Its sleek animal print was a mix of masculine and feminine, not exactly cross-dressing, but somewhere in between. Maybe, in its ambiguity, ten years later, when every trendy straight guy with a septum piercing and a ukulele calls themselves queer, it might be labeled gender-fluid. And maybe, fifty years earlier, the police would have thrown me into a paddy wagon: men and trans women caught waltzing in clothing perceived to be designed for cis women could be arrested in New York for "impersonating a female" as recently as 2011. I didn't think about the awkward time in history I inhabited as I held it out in front of me—around the corner from being able to freely experiment with style, a few steps ahead of being arrested for the same thing. I liked it, so I put it on.

"Yeah, it's nice," said Miss Andry when I did a little spin

for her at that night's rehearsal. "But you know you have to take that shit off, right?"

She was right. It was one thing to feel comfortable around people who'd proved they would support me unconditionally, but if I wanted to be a good stripper, I had to figure out how to feel sexy *naked* . . . and around strangers who didn't care about my feelings. All afternoon, I'd worked on a new routine in my bedroom. This one would be less cliché than the number I'd ripped off from the men on YouTube. I drew inspiration from weirdos who oozed sensuality without compromising themselves—David Bowie, Bianca Jagger, Selena—and decided to try treating sexiness as a ritual, something I had to summon, rather than a quality everyone inherently was born with. Those times I'd felt repulsive, it wasn't because I was. The boy's father pulling his son away. Eric calling my bleached hair "interesting." I wasn't the problem. They'd butchered my magic.

With the troupe's help that night and over the next three weeks of rehearsal, I practiced dancing and believing, as embarrassed as the words made me, that my new routine was sexy. The relentless positive-affirmations gimmick still felt a little phony to me, but not as phony as keeping constant watch over myself to make sure I didn't scare anyone off by being too femme.

"You are sexy!" the members of Polylust screamed, whether I tripped or forgot a step or had a wardrobe malfunction. In their world it seemed there was no way *not* to be sexy. With them the word lost its exclusivity, the rare quality that I believed made it special. I wasn't sure how to feel about that at first. We use words to define things, to separate. A dog is not a cat is not a Fabergé egg. Everything couldn't be sexy, because then nothing would be. It needed to mean something specific, otherwise how would I know what it was? Yet when I screamed "You are sexy!" to Arturo or Maya or Joanie, it meant something different every time. Arturo's graceful movements were sexy. Maya's rebelliousness. Joanie's boldness. Telling them so didn't weaken the word. It didn't affect my own self-esteem. I wasn't lying. If they thought they were sexy, then they were, and that had nothing do with me and my definition of it.

With Eric, I never truly felt sexy. I felt protected, which was the more urgent priority. Dressing down to fit into his version of attractiveness freed me of the target taped to my back. That gave me a certain type of confidence that could temporarily pass for happiness. Part of me yearned to know that freedom again, but I was gradually understanding that feigning masculinity wasn't freedom, not really. How free could I be if I was with someone more out of fear than desire? What kind of freedom did I have if I was constantly afraid of being caught?

I didn't have the answers yet, but at The Space, I was learning it was okay to ask the questions.

Polylust's $150 performance fee barely covered the gas to make it to Fort Myers, the town a two-hour drive from Orlando

where we were booked to perform. Our low pay was a tradeoff
we were willing to accept. Unlike career strippers, the hair-
less girls who actually made money taking off their clothes,
we didn't expect to pay our rent dancing. We had permission
from our empty bank accounts to waddle onstage, bloated
and mostly untrained, and do whatever we wanted.

Lillith DeVille steered our borrowed minivan, the
baby-doll-head earrings she'd worn to my first rehearsal
swaying in the breeze of the air conditioner, while Joanie, in
the passenger seat next to her, tried to convince the rest of
the troupe to try one of the lukewarm boiled peanuts she'd
bought from a man and his dog at a wooden stand on the
side of the road. The van's two back rows—where Arturo,
Miss Terry Machine, Miss Andry, and I were crammed
along with our suitcases of props and costumes—groaned.
Joanie promised we'd pull over for a real meal at the nearest
sign of life.

In the meantime, I stuck my head out the window and
gawked at the foreign landscape like I was on safari. We'd
opted to take the scenic route to Fort Myers, not realizing
until we were on the highway that the scenery would be
megachurches and graphic antiabortion billboards. Arturo
filled his time "bird watching."

"Truck Nutz!" he shouted, pointing at yet another
pair of plastic human testicles dangling from the rear of a
pickup truck, as common in these parts as confederate flags.
I sketched the nutz in a notebook, and we all took turns
guessing which one of us their owners would like to murder

most. The pansexual educator brainwashing the youth? The gay child of a Central American immigrant? Our laughter disguised our growing panic as the afternoon faded to black. This was the Bermuda Triangle of Florida, where queer people mysteriously disappeared.

When the GPS signaled we'd arrived at the venue, a gay bar called the Bottom Line, the troupe sighed with relief. The concrete building looked plain on the outside, but it had to be a sanctuary, like so many small-town gay bars. As the van approached, I wondered what went on behind its closed doors. Would the gay men inside be the kind who wrote "Masc 4 Masc" on their Grindr profiles? Or would they be the opposite—flaming country queens, up-to-date on all the latest beard moisturizers? After all, this was one of the few places around where they might feel comfortable displaying their queerness. Maybe they'd be a mixture of both. That gay men can either be femme or masc was a strict binary I'd become skeptical of after spending time with the women of Polylust, who shrugged off those labels, which were too limiting to describe their complex identities. Lillith, for one, didn't care to add up the individual parts of her outfits to figure out what side of the gender spectrum she landed on. Did her Dr. Martens combat boots cancel out her pearls? And were her baby-doll-head earrings masculine or feminine? Spending time with her helped me see how inadequate those categories could be. Regardless of the troupe's ideas about gender, the binary thrived in nightclubs, where hungry eyes looked you up and down to peg you as a top or a bottom, a stud or a stem, and I was curious if and how I'd be judged at the Bottom Line, whether I'd done a good job hiding that I was a swarm of bats in a trench coat.

Before I could find out, Joanie spotted a restaurant across the street, one of those throwback diners where waiters are required to wear bowties and little white caps in the shape of origami canoes. She decided to make a pit stop there first. Inside, Arturo and I sucked down our milkshakes quickly and rushed to the bathroom. The show was scheduled to begin in a little over two hours, and we wanted to get a head start putting on our costumes since, in addition to helping the girls with theirs at the bar, we'd also have to make the stage floor cottage-cheese-proof.

We took over a stall and stripped off our sweatpants and tank tops. Arturo threaded his feet into a white jockstrap and a pair of denim cut-off shorts. I pulled on a pair of briefs I'd bedazzled with the word *KISS* and carefully buttoned on my tear-away track pants. The fluorescent lighting made our reflections look haggard, especially after the long minivan ride. Painting our lips red and patting glitter on our cheeks and temples brought our faces back to life. We slipped on our performance tops: a guayabera shirt for Arturo's salsa-inspired dance, and a white button-up shirt encrusted with metal studs for me.

As I glued star-shaped pasties with yellow fringe over my nipples, Arturo stared into the mirror, tapping his chin with his index finger.

"It's missing something," he said. He reached into his book

bag and pulled out a bottle of gold hairspray, misting it over himself until his entire body sparkled like a trophy. "There." He took one last look at his reflection. "*That's* Havana Gold."

His confidence was contagious, and though I only saw myself in the mirror, not Johnny Deep, we both emerged from the bathroom with our shiny heads held up.

Now that we were dressed in our flashy burlesque costumes, the walk back to the troupe's table stretched on for miles. I tucked my arms into my sides and trailed behind Arturo, realizing the mistake we'd made. Every laugh, every comment whispered into an ear, had the unmistakable edge of people planning a mutiny. How could I have been so naïve as to think it'd be fine to dress so flamboyantly here, in a diner that romanticized an era when people like us were jailed for holding hands in public? There was confidence and there was recklessness. Arturo pranced ahead of me, seemingly oblivious. His composure drove me to paranoia. Was I making up that father wrapping his arm around his young son, or was that an earlier memory imposing itself on the present? Was the line cook shaking his head at the patties on the grill because of us, or was he overworked and adding up the hours left on his shift? When we finally reached the table, Arturo slid in next to Joanie. I followed, taking a seat beside Miss Terri Machine—no, just Megan—any magic I'd felt in the bathroom eclipsed by reality.

Here's what you don't know, if you want to feel sexy: You don't know there are hit songs on the radio with lyrics about killing you. You don't remember the teacher in high school who laughed along when your classmate asked how you and your boyfriend dealt with "the shit." You ignore that there are still laws barring sodomy. You never received electro-shock therapy, so desperate parents willing to try anything might as well not be real. You don't go back to the bedroom your uncle locked you in with a woman, back when you were thirteen and still played with lizards. The statistics about LGBT homelessness are only numbers to you. The pink tri-angles worn by queers in concentration camps are just shapes. Learning of the murder of Matthew Shepard, that his killers assaulted a pair of Latino teenagers immediately afterward, which was when it first became clear you could be hated for both your skin and the person who lived underneath it, just seems like trivia. You flip the channel on the morning talk shows when the subject turns to "What would you do if your child came out as gay?" You run outside and catch a friend.

Here's how you talk: in perfectly. Enunciated. English.

Here's what you do: nothing, I told myself. Don't be so dramatic. You don't have to do anything. You're in public. No one is going to try anything here.

Forget about all the times queer people have been at-tacked in public.

You're with friends.

Forget that most people are not your friend.

"Just in case," the bartender at Savoy had once told me about the shotgun above the register.

I wrapped my fingers around a butter knife. Just in case what?

What's the worst that could happen? No one was going to attack me at a diner. And if they tried, Arturo could flip over our table to deflect the bullets. I imagined that, imagined myself ripping off my tear-away pants to use as a tourniquet. Joanie could seal our wounds with candle wax. Megan had enough cottage cheese in her purse to last us a few days. Miss Andry was good for creating a distraction with her bucket of green goo, giving Lillith DeVille enough time to run outside and pull up in our getaway van. The more impossible the scene, the less real the eyes digging into my skull felt. I set the knife down, took a deep breath.

"You look good," Megan said, stabbing a fry into a puddle of ketchup. "Selfie?"

The first picture was bad; so was the second. We tried again until we were both happy.

Two hours later, Joanie ran offstage with a fistful of crumpled dollar bills as the final notes of "Personal Jesus" faded out.

"You're gonna kill!" she screamed, slinking behind the curtain that led to the greenroom. Moments earlier, I'd watched her perform the same routine that had hypnotized me the first time I caught Polylust at The Space, when I was awestruck by the idea that a person could expose themselves to a room full of strangers and demand admiration—beyond that, that there were people who wanted more from life than to simply feel safe.

It was my turn, and I still wasn't ready. After the glares at the diner, any curiosity I'd had about the crowd at the Bottom Line was gone. This place looked like every gay bar everywhere: neon lights rippled along the walls; men in trucker caps were perched over the bar like turtles on a rock. Why would anything be different here?

I stepped onto the hot white stage. A few people cheered as they recognized the funky opening chords of "Kiss." Their applause drowned out Prince's first words about not having to be beautiful to turn him on.

In front of me, instead of the audience, my eyes could only make out a thick wall of black. I took a moment to let my irises adapt to the spotlight. A second turned into five. Still the faces in the crowd were veiled in darkness. Legs shaking, I swayed from side to side, not sure who I was dancing for or what they were thinking. Was this what Joanie saw? And Arturo and Miss Terri Machine and the rest of the troupe? Nothing?

There were no eyes widening in awe. No one to demand admiration from.

I pried apart the buttons of my shirt, noticing another strange absence. No one was looking at me like I disgusted them, not anyone I could see, anyway. I might as well have been alone in my bedroom, rubbing lotion into my arms and stripping in front of a mirror. I'd felt sexy then, behind my closed door. So that was where I told myself I was.

"Nice tits!" someone yelled as I tore my shirt open, revealing the pasties underneath. A balled-up dollar landed by my feet. More followed as I hopped and whipped the yellow tassels around in circles. By the time I finished the trick, my legs were relaxed, my chest slick with sweat. Part of me was turned on by the anonymity of the audience. Anyone could be out there, watching.

I strutted around the stage trailing my fingers along the edge of my pants. Screams came from everywhere and nowhere as I ripped them off and turned around, the bright-pink *KISS* on my briefs sparkling under the spotlight.

"Yes, bitch!" a mousy voice called out.

I slapped my ass and faced the crowd again. Ran my hand down my chest, followed my happy trail into my briefs. When Prince launched into his guitar solo, I pulled out a pick from my crotch, dropped to my knees, and played my bulge like a Fender Telecaster.

I didn't know how anyone else did it. Joanie and the rest of the troupe. It could be that they were effortlessly confident. It could be that spirits took over their bodies when they danced. Or maybe they did what I did. They found a place in their minds where it was okay to be sexy, where they were safe, and they carried it with them.

After the show, Polylust took over the dance floor. Tipsy on our free-drink tickets, we sweated off our makeup lip-syncing along to divas the DJ spun, it seemed, just for us. I giggled watching my gang of freaks jump-cutting under the strobe lights frame by frame like a movie reel. This feeling—of belonging, being cute—probably wouldn't last, so I pulled Arturo in.

"You're sexy!" I yelled at him.

"Shut up." He blushed and jabbed my shoulder. "You are!"

There was no pressure to believe each other, no false promises that this was true. For now it was enough that we were together, in a place where we could be whoever we wanted to be, and to hope that someday we could summon this feeling again.

There Used to Be a Gay Bar

On Christmas Day in Orlando, Hector and I drove through empty, festive streets, looking for someplace open to eat. Palm trees wrapped in red-and-white tinsel lined the sides of the road ahead. Say something, I thought. Though he was only three years older than my twenty-four, every attempt to talk felt clumsy and forced. We were like old friends from high school, forced to make small talk after bumping into each other at the grocery store. I racked my brain for a conversation topic. It didn't have to be good. Anything. I just had to say anything at all.

A dumb joke would work: "So, you've been MIA."

"Yeah," he could answer. "In Miami."

Hector moved there for college the same year I started high school at Oak Ridge, and I'd only seen him a handful of times since. It wasn't laugh-out-loud funny, but maybe it'd be enough to get the ball rolling. Next to me, he steered with his knees, scrolling through playlists on his phone with one hand and tapping a carton of cigarettes on his thigh with the other. He flicked the lid open under my nose. I shook my head no, then leaned out my window, taking in the spectacle of Christmas in Florida. Elves in swim trunks were piled into sales bins outside Dollar General. Locals wearing Santa hats and sunglasses carried cases of Bud Light Lime out.

I'd only moved to California in September, but already the streets here looked alien. We drove by a McDonald's where the menu sign outside read "We are a PokéStop," and directly below, "#OrlandoStrong," the hashtag that dominated vigils and billboards in the days after the Pulse nightclub shooting. It'd been six months since the attack. Six, and we were downgraded to a McDonald's menu. Six more and we'd be pushed out to herald the return of the McRib.

"You good?" Hector asked. He landed on a country song I'd never heard before and drummed his fingers against the steering wheel, the edges of his nails crusty with dirt from working on construction sites. A smile spread across his face, as if the singer brought him back good memories. To me it sounded like every other country song. A cowboy was sad. A woman was a horse. What was this? Hector's iPod used to be filled with Nicaraguan punk bands that railed against the Sandinista dictatorship. Reggaeton music about having sex on the kitchen floor. I cringed, watching him lip-sync with his eyes closed. The long lashes we'd both inherited from our father were the only familiar thing left about him. He'd filled out since we'd last seen each other. Two of my arms could fit inside one of his shirt sleeves, and his thick chest looked like a podium holding up his round, bald head. Our cousins used to call him Maracas when we were little. We'd shake him and dance to the imaginary salsa music his brain knocking around his skull made. Now he was singing about going to honky-tonks? What the hell was a honky-tonk? And when and where did he find out?

"Yeah, I'm good," I said. I wanted my mom.

We were back in town to spend the holiday with her. Except, in our family, someone is always dying. The night before, it was my stepdad's mother. Mom took a last-minute red-eye to Mexico for the funeral. Hector had already driven up from Miami. I'd flown in from California, and my return flight wasn't for another week. Seven more days of this. We were going to have to figure out a way to talk without our mother to curate our conversations.

"Why don't you two go to the movies?" she'd suggested before leaving. We nodded politely, our only shared interest our disinterest in spending time together.

"We'll be fine," we'd told her.

Hector scratched his knee and exhaled plumes of smoke out his window.

After a moment, I suggested Anthony's Pizza, the restaurant downtown with the new mural featuring a flock of forty-nine doves representing the shooting victims. Polylust used to rehearse in the empty studio apartment above it. The Space. To think I'd been learning to dance without fear.

"No," he said.

"What about Zaza?" I tried; it was a Cuban diner a block from Mom's house.

"No," he repeated.

"Is there anywhere you want to go?" I sank into my seat, feeling starved and ridiculous in my Hawaiian shirt and flip-flops. My clothes gave away the trip I wished this had been. Light and breezy. Somehow I'd forgotten how cold it gets in Florida, that some years the temperature drops so low iguanas freeze and fall from the trees. I'd forgotten what Hector was like.

"Not really." He turned up his white-boy music.

We'd been driving for nearly twenty minutes when we came to a stop at a red light. Across the street, a group of people were gathered outside a white building. It took me a second—long enough that now, years later, I wonder if I didn't want to see it—but at last the realization of where we were smacked me dumb. Pulse. Next door, four hands spelled out the word *love* in sign language on the wall of an Einstein Bros. Bagels.

It's sacrilege among Orlando queers, but I hadn't visited the site yet. I'd donated money for the displaced workers, stood in solidarity with the survivors at several vigils, yet I had not been able to bring myself to visit the building, which was in limbo between crime scene and memorial.

Going to a gay bar while the sun was out felt wrong,

like catching a drag queen under fluorescent lights. Pulse already had a place in my memories, where it firmly existed cloaked in the nighttime. That was how I chose to remember it. It's where I spent my eighteenth birthday, my twenty-first, buying an all-you-can-drink wristband for twenty dollars and chugging well Long Islands until I puked. If it wasn't going to be *that* Pulse anymore, what was the point? So I abstained, saving face with my friends by telling them I'd already gone on my own.

What was there to see? The hole in the wall where the police set off explosives? The bathroom where Omar Mateen held my people hostage, taking forty-nine lives before putting a gun to his head? When I left for California, it was partly because I didn't want to stay in the city long enough to watch the bar become another cheap roadside attraction.

From Hector's car, I watched throngs of mourners gathered around the club. Who were they? Family? Friends? Tourists? Probably a combination of all three. Blown-up photos of the victims flanked the entrances, but otherwise the place looked like it had gone wild. Elaborate flower bouquets littered the parking lot. Lilies and roses lay in stacks, weighing down posters with messages to the deceased. "Love cannot be killed" and "We won't let hate win" and the only one that felt particularly true: "We miss you." I looked at Hector, curious if he'd taken this road on purpose. He stared ahead waiting for the light to turn.

I'd called him the night after the shooting, blacked out outside of Parliament House, where an impromptu vigil had formed. If I hadn't been drunk, I might have let my anger at him for not calling me first fester, but the alcohol gave me the nerve to dial. He didn't answer, so I left a mortifying voicemail ending with "Maybe next time check in on your little brother after the deadliest mass shooting in modern US history?" The next day, he responded with a text: *Sorry, dude, I thought you were okay.*

I don't know what I was thinking. Of course he didn't call. I'd never told him I was gay. It's one of the few things I assumed he knew about me without me having to say it. Him reaching out to me would have been a breach in our unspoken contract about not discussing my sexuality. Perhaps he thought he was doing me a favor. I would have been as uncomfortable with it as him. Yet, in the hours between the shooting and my voicemail, I'd had complete strangers embrace me, acquaintances I hadn't spoken to in years offer their condolences. None of it meant anything if the person I knew the most and the longest couldn't be bothered. After Pulse, more than ever, I needed Hector to say the obvious thing out loud: I don't care that you're gay. I love you. Once would have been enough. I am a love camel. I would have made that last.

Across the road, a toddler waddled back and forth between the memorial photos on the ground. I leaned back in my seat and wondered if Hector was thinking about my drunk call. It would be typical of our relationship: the two of us sitting side by side, privately replaying something I'd said months earlier, both too nervous to bring it up.

Even so, I allowed myself a masochistic fantasy. Maybe he was finally going to act like my big brother. The past few years, which we'd lived in near silence, could be reset. Things were different now. I could have been *there*. I could not be *here*. Maybe he wasn't going to say it, but he would show me he loved me by taking me to Pulse. I couldn't do it alone, but with him it might be bearable. I kept my excitement hidden, not wanting to spoil his surprise.

The light turned green. I mentally prepared for our arrival. Suddenly I had a million things to tell him, starting with *Asshole, you could have given me a heads-up*. I would have bought flowers, worn something that didn't have a hula dancer on it. I couldn't believe I was going in flip-flops. How many hours had I spent finessing my outfits when it was still Pulse, the bar with the cutest boys, who looked you up and down before deciding if you were worth it? I was caught up in the pageantry, worried I was wearing the wrong thing, not bringing the appropriate offering. Without me noticing, he had turned the car in the opposite direction of the club. We were headed away from downtown, his eyes fixed intensely on the road, hands at ten and two.

Don't say anything, I thought. It doesn't matter. You didn't want to go anyway. My disappointment hung in the air before I quickly swallowed it again. In the rearview mirror, Pulse got smaller, shrinking into a pale white dot before it finally disappeared.

·

Fifteen years before the shooting, fourteen-year-old Omar Mateen was enrolled at Spectrum Alternative School, a disciplinary campus for students with behavioral issues. Things like fighting, cutting class. Spectrum wasn't so much a school as a threat: keep acting out and you know where you'll end up. If at that age he was interested in men, he never told his father, Seddique Mateen. Like me, he would have been terrified about telling anyone at all. The Mateens were a pious family, offering regular generous donations to a local mosque they attended, though at Spectrum, Omar did little to outwardly express his Islamic faith. He slipped his religion off at the door, surrendering to the more powerful life force of high school and his desire to be liked.

He wasn't. Former classmates looking for words to describe him settled on "chubby." Others recall him getting slapped in the back of the head while riding the bus to campus each morning. He was one of very few students of Afghan descent, standing out in the suburb of Stuart, Florida, where in the 2000 census, over 80 percent of the population reported as identifying as "white alone." In an interview with *The Washington Post*, Spectrum alumnus Justin Delancey spoke about Omar being brutally bullied: "He'd try to joke and laugh and make fun of himself to get the attention off." It was an old trick. Turning your harasser's words on yourself so they think you don't care. "But it didn't work."

On September 11, 2001, he tried again. His classmates remember that watching the Twin Towers collapse on a small classroom television that morning, Omar couldn't stop smiling. Was he delighted by the sight of gray figures jumping off the buildings into clouds of smoke and debris, or was he already worried students would link the brown faces on the television with his brown skin, the grin masking his nerves? Reporters looking for a connection between Omar's early history and the Pulse shooting uncovered a progress report dating back to the fifth grade. On it, a teacher noted that Mateen "lacks remorse." I'm curious, knowing the way minorities are dehumanized in this country, what it means for an elementary school student to lack remorse. What would have been an appropriate response to terrorism for a child who must have understood that the images flashing onscreen would ruin the lives of so many in his community?

"It was almost, like, surreal how happy he was about what happened to us," another classmate told *The Washington Post*. Reportedly, Mateen began to brag that Osama bin Laden was his uncle, spinning a tale about how the founder of Al-Qaeda taught him how to shoot an AK-47 when he was younger. Before September 11, most teenagers did not know who Osama bin Laden was, so it's likely Omar seized the name from the news coverage to fabricate his story. If making fun of himself didn't work, he could use the terrorist attacks to his advantage. Make himself look tough, connected. Students grew angry. At Spectrum, this was no minor risk. Mateen's teacher sent him to the dean's office. His father was summoned to pick him up. When he arrived, the older man slapped his son across the face in the courtyard in full sight of his classmates. Perhaps, predicting the rise in hate crimes against Muslims that were soon to come, Seddique wanted to distance his family from the attacks. They were not terrorists, the slap articulated to those who witnessed it. The Mateens loved America.

How could he ever return to class now? His classmates despised him. His father saw him as a liability. He was on the bottom rung at a school where students were sent when they failed everywhere else. Pulse, a place where he could one day escape, was a two-hour drive away.

I don't have sympathy for the man who murdered forty-nine people I used to dance with. I promise you I don't. But I do for the child he'd been, despite knowing how this story ends, because he reminds me so much of myself.

Like him, I was easy to spot as a freshman at Boone, the only Latinx kid in my criminal justice program. Before starting high school, during the trip to Nicaragua, I had finally admitted to myself that I was attracted to other boys. Petrified, with no one I could ask for help or guidance, I clung to the one silver lining: back in Orlando I knew exactly what I needed to do to hide. If journalists dug through my high school records, what would they find? On one progress report, a teacher wrote: "Edgar is lovely to have in class. I wish he would communicate more." Would a journalist reading that understand I was afraid people could sniff the gay on me? That I was too scared to be seen after a classmate referred to my just-coming-in beard as "spic hair," too afraid to speak because someone might notice my lisp, my faint accent? I skipped lunch every day and fell asleep in a bathroom stall on campus, where I didn't have to worry about what anyone thought of how I spoke, or dressed, or where I came from. I wasn't bullied, but only because I made myself invisible.

At home, Hector occasionally called me a fag. Every brother I knew used that word to tease their siblings. Still, out of his lips it sounded like a warning. I could tell by the way he kept me far from his friends that he was embarrassed by me. I watered my appearance down and tried to build a case, if not for my being straight, then for plausible deniability in the event that things ever really got bad. The program was the perfect cover. I traded in my skinny jeans for military fatigues and combat boots. Buzzing my hair meant there was nothing to fuss over in the mornings. I wasn't myself at home, or at school. I knew if anyone found out about me, things would just get worse. Asleep in the bathroom, I dreamt of rich men coming to save me.

Somehow I got close with a boy in French, the one class where I was required to speak. Colton was a rich white kid, the type who thought owning a Biggie album made him tough. I imagine he read my silence as hardness. We smoked weed together behind the mall on weekends, lying on the cool patch of grass under trees using our skateboards as headrests. It wasn't much, nothing compared to what Pulse would be to me in the years to come. But for an hour or two I could look at a cloud and fade away.

Here is where my life and Omar's shift out of sync. After

Colton was caught dealing and the two of us were expelled, I could have, like Omar, been sent to a behavioral school or juvie. Instead, because the superintendent wiped my record clean, I was sent to Oak Ridge, the school my neighborhood was zoned for. In retrospect the expulsion turned out to be a blessing. Within the course of a few months, I went from being the only queer Latinx person in class to being surrounded by kids who looked like me. And I met Angel. That same year, Hector left for Miami, relieving some of the pressure on me to perform masculinity. Though I still treaded lightly around Mom and my stepdad, I slowly learned to speak again. A handful of supportive teachers and fiercely protective girls at Oak Ridge made my eighteenth birthday seem within reach.

When I made it to Pulse, I finally understood what it meant to have my life belong to me. It was there that I tried karaoke for the first time, tripping over the words to Dolly Parton's "9 to 5" and spilling a little of my vodka cranberry at each chorus. On other nights, I danced the Time Warp, flirted with men, slapped away hands reaching for my ass. It wasn't the prettiest club. The music sucked before midnight. Parking was hell. But it was open Thanksgiving, Halloween, Christmas. Hector visited Mom and me for the first couple of these holidays after he moved, and each time we had less and less to talk about as so many of my new experiences were inextricable from my queerness. How could I tell him about Princess, or Polylust, or who I was dating without telling him I was gay? It was easier to leave things unsaid.

Reading about Omar Mateen's early life, I'm disturbed by the similarities we shared as teenagers. My depression and self-hate could have manifested themselves in any number of ways if my record hadn't gotten wiped away by the superintendent, or if I'd never become friends with Colton and stayed on at Boone. Omar is dead. In the absence of a trial where he would have been cross-examined, I crave a physical map of his life I can spread out before me so that I may point and say, *That* is when someone could have stepped in. *There* is where the world could have given him hope. Because I don't know how we can survive this happening again.

Hector and I arrived at Anthony's Pizza, long after I had suggested it. The restaurant is located in a prime corner of Mills 50, the Orlando arts district where you can take a Jazzercise class, drink boba tea, and buy a necklace to ward off the evil eye, all within one block. It was Christmas, so the parking lot was deserted. Hector, all of a sudden eager for pizza, took up two spaces with his Jeep.

"Is this the place?" He turned off the radio.

"I thought you didn't want to come here," I shot back, frustrated that he couldn't agree to come here in the first place. He stepped out of the car and headed for the front door without saying a word. As usual, I followed.

I've always wondered where he got his masculinity from. As children, Hector and I had fairly similar interests in cartoons and gaudy jewelry. We often barricaded ourselves in our room and eavesdropped on my stepdad arguing with Mom about how she was raising us—arguments that gradually morphed into discussions about me, why she was letting me walk like that, bleach my hair, all euphemisms for what he really meant to ask: Why are you letting your son be gay? Around that time something changed, and Hector became a model son, obsessed with girls and sports.

Perhaps attempting to deflect the attention off me, he postured himself as everything I wasn't. There was only room for so much femininity between two boys, and as I used up my portion, he gave me his.

Or maybe he wasn't protecting me but Mom. When he came home after soccer and rugby practice with bruises on his arms and legs, he proved she wasn't doing a bad job raising us. Clearly, the pools of blue and purple on his body said, we had the capacity to be men. It wasn't her fault, like our stepdad implied. It was me who was defective.

I'm sure if I asked him, Hector would roll his eyes and say he simply liked rugby.

Whatever the reason, when I looked at him at Anthony's, I saw a clone of the men in our family. For the first fifteen minutes after ordering our food, he barely said a word.

"You're doing a really good Omar impression," I told him.

He dropped his eyes down to his plate, zeroing in on his meal.

Omar is our stepdad, the man who rarely spoke to us beyond a grunt, and who, of course, shares a name with Omar

Mateen. As with all stepparents since the dawn of fairy tales, there's no version of this story where it wasn't always going to be him against me.

Once, after Hector had gone away to college, I over-heard Omar and Mom fighting. It sounded physical. This time, I didn't have my brother with me to turn up the volume on the radio. Overcome by a sudden sense of duty—as, I guess, the new "man of the house"—I stormed into their bedroom. She was sitting on the bed with her face in her hands. Omar was standing above her. "Leave," I told him. Mom wiped the tears from her face and asked me to go to my room. His father had passed away that afternoon. This was not the time for me to insert myself, she said.

But it was too late. I'd never interrupted one of their fights. Never defended her. It felt too good to stop. I kept at it, unwavering in my insistence that he go, pointing a finger in his face, daring him.

He shoved me out of the way, knocking me backward onto a dresser. Without thinking, I jumped to my feet and swung. He landed in a heap on the floor. It was so easy.

And yet the punch knocked something else out of place too. The miserable old man I hit bore no resemblance to the person who had made me question myself from the day I met him. His thinning white hair. Dark circles under his eyes, still red either from drinking or crying over his dead father or both. I hovered over him with my fist. This was exactly what he'd wanted from me as a child, and it was what I wanted right then, but I didn't feel any satisfaction. I felt absurd. See how stupid we look, I wanted to tell him. Whatever we're doing here is bad for all of us.

"I'm going to tell everyone you pushed me," I shouted instead, hoping to scare him off before the fight escalated any further.

Mom pulled him up by his elbow. "Who are you going to call?" he laughed, staggering to his feet. "Your dad? Your uncles? Please. Do it. No one is going to come for *you*."

There it was. What I had been denying to myself for years, so casually stated. It was blood that connected me to the rest of my family, not love. No one would come if I called, and we all knew it. Why would they? Had they ever helped me before? The only person who ever came close was Hector. Whenever our cousins asked me about girlfriends, he'd shake his maraca head and we'd laugh so hard everyone forgot what we were talking about.

I was wrong. Hector was not Omar, not my uncles. There was more between us than blood.

Hector stabbed his eggplant parmesan. "The food here is so heavy."

"So heavy!" I yelped, pretending my pizza weighed fifteen pounds. He didn't laugh.

Though he works in construction now, when we were younger Hector wanted to be a director. He'd cast me in our home movies as the female villains, the tearful ingénues. Because we did it together, our family couldn't decide whether to be horrified or giggle when we held screenings. Still, every few months, he calls to pitch me a new project: "Hey, little bro, I have an idea for a screenplay about a cabana boy. Think Will Ferrell." "Sup, broski, I need you to write me a movie. I'm securing the funds. I want a comedy. Big bucks." "Hey, man, I'm thinking about moving to Italy. Don't tell Mom."

On the phone, he comes to life. But in person, we flatline.

I wanted to bring out Phone Hector. Real-Life Hector stared blankly at the football game on one of the restaurant's televisions.

"How's work?" I asked him.

"Solid," he said.

"Still live in that place near South Beach?"

"Yes."

"Whatever happened to moving to Italy?"

"The food's so heavy here."

The last time we were together was years ago, for my college graduation. Like I said, in our family, someone is always dying. The night before the ceremony it was my grandmother. My mother's hands were tied. She had to go. I couldn't afford a plane ticket to the funeral in Nicaragua.

"Take pictures for me," Mom said, throwing random articles of clothing into her suitcase. It had been minutes since she'd answered the call from my uncle telling her my grandmother was found on the floor of her bathroom. I counted six pairs of socks in her luggage for her planned two-day stay. When she wasn't looking, I shoved clean underwear inside.

Then too, Hector drove up to Orlando from Miami. Then too, we sat at restaurants trying to figure out what to say to each other. On the day of the ceremony, I painted my nails purple to go with my gown and sat in my assigned seat, next to a girl who kept waving at someone in the audience. Omar had work, and I didn't bother asking him to request time off. Most of my family was in Miami. We couldn't speak to each other, but at least I knew that somewhere in the arena was Hector, even if our minds were off in Nicaragua.

I sobbed, letting the tears roll freely down my cheeks. I wondered if at that exact moment Mom was crying at the funeral, if Hector was crying for my grandmother too. Why didn't he go? I may not have had the money, but he did. I searched for his face in the stands, asking myself why he didn't leave me behind, though I knew the answer.

At Anthony's, I drew circles with a straw among the grease stains in my paper plate. Hector was hunched over his meal, elbows on the table. He shoveled bites of eggplant into his mouth, chewing each forkful slowly.

The thought of walking out entered my mind. I didn't mean to laugh, but imagining myself standing up, exiting the restaurant with no explanation, and taking a cab home was funny to me. He'd be left sitting there alone, trying to figure out what he'd done. Maybe only then would he realize he'd done nothing, and it was this nothing—what seemed like a complete disinterest in my hurt, in me—that crushed me. He lifted his eyes and held them to mine, as if he thought it was him that I was laughing at and he wanted me to see how much he didn't care. It wasn't him. It was the impossible situation we were in: if I asked him to take me to Pulse, we'd have to acknowledge my queerness, and that might create more distance between us. If I didn't, we would continue in this nothingness. I didn't know which was worse. It was funny to think there was no way out of this mess we'd created. Nothing to do about our nothing but laugh.

Finally he wiped his mouth with a napkin and threw it triumphantly on his plate.

"Heavy," he said. "So, where in California do you live?"

"Riverside," I said.

"Near L.A., right?"

I nodded.

"Solid."

Back in the car, he asked if I wanted to go see a movie. It wasn't Pulse. Or I love you. But it was two more hours together.

"Okay," I said.

In retrospect, it's a miracle anyone ever comes out of the closet, considering all of the ways the world tells queer people to deny ourselves. Of course Omar Mateen would have never admitted to having same-sex attractions. Of course he was filled with hate. But so was I, and I didn't buy a fucking assault rifle. Now that the harm has been done, my concern isn't with absolving the man. I want to know when Omar could have been stopped, because he is not the only one to blame.

After graduating from high school, he hopped from job

to job, never staying in one place for too long. His résumé doesn't seem to point to any larger aim. He worked as a bagger at a popular Southern grocery store chain, followed by stints at Chick-fil-A, Circuit City, Walgreens, Hollister Co., and the supplement store General Nutrition Centers (GNC). Some colleagues described him as fun, always chasing after girls. Others suggested Omar lived a double life.

Samuel King, who was a year ahead of Omar in high school, worked at the Ruby Tuesday restaurant next door to GNC at the mall. King, who performed in drag at night, told *The Daily Beast* that Omar would occasionally hang out with his group of openly gay friends, often sitting at the bar after a shift, where he joked around with the lesbian bartenders. Omar's former manager at GNC, Margaret Barone, whom Mateen called "Miss Margaret," simply assumed he was gay. Another gay man, David Gonzalez, told *The Washington Post* that he remembers how Omar used to look at him "in a certain way like he wanted me to approach him." Gonzalez, who lived next door to Mateen's parents, said, "He knew I was gay."

Nearly a decade before the shooting, Omar began to take serious interest in transforming his appearance. Already six feet tall, he used his employee discount to purchase protein powders and supplements from GNC, bulking up so quickly that he developed stretch marks on his skin. He was done being used as an example. He was nineteen now and planned to become a police officer. Had I graduated from Boone's criminal justice program, I might have been doing the same. After earning his associate's degree in criminal justice technology from Indian River State College, he quit his job in search of work that would put him closer to law enforcement. He found employment as a correctional officer at a state prison, swearing under oath to "perform my duties faithfully and in accordance with my mission to ensure the public safety." In April of 2007, the same month as the Virginia Tech massacre and less than a year after he was hired, Omar was dismissed. Colleagues suspect it had something to do with him asking a classmate at the police training academy whether he would report him if he brought a gun to campus, though no formal charges were made.

Five months later, with a clean record, he found a new job at G4S, a leading U.S. security firm, where he was still working the night of the shooting. According to a statement released by G4S, "Mateen was subject to detailed company screening when he was recruited in 2007 and rescreened in 2013 with no adverse findings." As a licensed security guard, Omar was granted a permit to carry a concealed weapon.

That same year, allegedly motivated by his coworkers teasing him about his Islamic faith, he bragged that he had family connections to Al-Qaeda and that he was a member of Hezbollah, echoing the stories he told as a teenager of being Osama bin Laden's nephew. Again, he was turning his peers' biases against them: Al-Qaeda and Hezbollah are bitter enemies, a fact Omar must have known his coworkers weren't aware of. It's possible he didn't know that himself. Even so, his claims landed him on an FBI watch list, and Mateen was placed in a terrorism database. After ten months of surveillance during which his calls and movements were tracked, the FBI determined he had only said those things "to try to freak out his co-workers." From claiming familial ties to Osama bin Laden to fabricating connections to rival Islamist militant groups and, later, inside the club, telling the police that the Boston bombers were his "homeboys," Omar was a skilled hand at playing to American fears. It was the only hand he knew he had.

Plausible deniability: in 2011, he married a woman he met online.

Plausible deniability: they had a child. A boy.

Plausible deniability: four days before the shooting, video footage shows Omar kneeling inside a mosque, praying.

It's evident that Omar, if not queer himself, was at least friendly with queer people, a wrench in his father's story that the shooting was motivated by an incident that occurred a few months earlier. "We were in downtown Miami. Bayside. People were playing music. And he saw two men kissing each other in front of his wife and kid and he got very angry," his father told reporters. Gay marriage had recently been declared legal in all fifty states, in June of 2015. "They were kissing each other and touching each other and he said, 'Look at that. In front of my son they are doing that.'" If Omar was never comfortable telling his father about his sexuality, why would Seddique have believed anything to the contrary? To admit knowing about Omar's hidden life would have been to acknowledge that he had a hand in stifling it, that he was partly responsible for the damaged man his son would grow up to be.

Free of the watchful eye of the FBI, with no open charges against him, Omar was legally able to purchase a handgun and a SIG Sauer MCX assault-style rifle in Port St. Lucie. The owner of the gun shop, a former New York City police officer who'd worked at the Twin Towers in the aftermath of the September 11 attacks, told reporters that if Omar "hadn't purchased them from us, I'm sure he would have gotten them from another local gun store in the area."

It could have been stopped when he was fired from the prison. It could have been stopped had he not been hired at G4S and granted a permit to carry a weapon. It could have been stopped when he was placed on the FBI terrorism watch list. It could have been stopped by his father. It could have been stopped at the gun store. It could have been stopped if at any point in his childhood he saw Pulse as a place that would have taken him in, like it did me, like it did so many of us.

On June 12, 2016, between 2:02 and 5:15 a.m., he walked into the bar. It was Latin Night, a busy Saturday that bled into early Sunday morning. The next day at Parliament House, I swallowed enough drinks to call Hector, because I knew he loved me. I just wanted to hear it.

I woke up the morning after Christmas and found Hector gone. Back to Miami and to us speaking on the phone every six months and "Yes, I'm fine, and I have an idea for a movie!" Mom, still in Mexico, extended her stay and wouldn't return until New Year's, leaving me with the house to myself.

I used to thrive in moments like these, home alone, coming alive the second Mom would step out to go to work. As soon as her car turned the street corner, I'd rush to her bathroom and dig through her makeup drawer. In my eagerness, I bypassed brushes and rubbed eyeshadow on my lids with my bare fingers, then twirled around in clouds of her rich floral perfume. Our bathroom was Pulse before I knew Pulse. When it was time for her to come back, I'd scrub the makeup off, take a shower, make myself invisible again. She wouldn't be returning from work this time. I could do anything.

I could go. After all, I didn't *need* Hector to take me. We were both grown now. Online I often saw pictures of him with his Miami friends. Getting an "I ♥ MOM" tattoo on his butt. Leaning over a giant margarita with his rugby team. He looked like the clown of the group, so different from the guy I saw in person. I don't know if I'm right, if he was so desperate to leave home because I'd sucked all the femininity out of the air, if he believed he had to make up for what I lacked in masculinity. In Miami, though, it seemed like he was getting to have his share, finding a happiness I had nothing to do with.

I sifted through the clean clothes in my suitcase. A pair of black jeans. A silk button-up shirt. Boots that could possibly pass as formal. Why not pay my respects?

I felt I owed the bar something. Pulse was the first place

where I didn't have to worry about being caught. Passing through its threshold, I shed any embarrassment I felt about being too girly, not liking the correct thing. There, we all liked the wrong thing.

As I stared down at my clothes, it hit me that I wasn't considering visiting the site because I thought it would make me feel better. I felt obligated. But what allegiance did I have to that building? It wasn't the walls that made Pulse feel like home; it was the people inside. It was them I was indebted to. No amount of flowers could even begin to pay them back. I wished there were a way for me to tell them what they meant, then realized there were some people who I still could.

I put on my outfit. Called some queer friends and had a potluck. We passed joints around, watched bad holiday movies. Some of us were out to our relatives, some not at all. Six months earlier we might have ended the night at the club. Whatever Pulse's legacy was—perhaps it's that for a few years, knowing it existed gave me a reason to hold on—I didn't need to visit its bricks to remember. In my memories, it's always Thanksgiving, Halloween, Christmas. My family is alive. They're dancing. A hand is pulling me toward them. We're free.

The Rest Is a Drag

Before I moved to California, before the trip back to Orlando, I was twenty-four years old and had a degree in creative writing, a twin-sized bed at my mother's house, and a job at a luxury flip-flop boutique at The Florida Mall. Which is to say I had the weekend, when I could forget all those things, go to Pulse, and pretend I was someone else.

Then one night, sometime around 3:00 a.m., Arturo called me, breathless.

"Thank God, you weren't there," he said.

"No," I answered when he finished talking a minute later. I hung up, turned over in bed. No, as if what he'd told me was up for debate.

A month after that, the shooting was everywhere. First the #OrlandoStrong signs went up on shop windows, then came the memorial T-shirts, followed by the heartbeat tattoos and the murals and the bumper stickers. A soccer stadium unveiled a rainbow section in the stands where you could eat a hot dog, watch a game, and simultaneously honor the victims. Online, a website started selling onesies for dogs with the slogan "Bark 4 Pulse." At a yard sale, a woman said she was proud of me, of *us*, then asked, with spectacular confidence, "Did any of your friends die?"

So, really, the shooting was everywhere. I couldn't deny it anymore.

And I was the best at that. Going to sleep when life became messy. Escaping. Whenever something was unbearable, I was great at not bearing it.

Instead I closed my eyes and went somewhere else, said, "No, not now," and put the thing that hurt aside for later. I didn't believe this made me a sociopath. Or that my inability to express my feelings in so-called healthier ways was typical machista bullshit. I believed it made me practical. Were I to break down whenever things got difficult, I'd never get anything done. For that reason, I kept my emotions locked in a room far back in my mind, and on a day I set aside for the purpose of airing them, I put on something light—a rom-com, or *RuPaul's Drag Race*—crawled into my warm TV screen like a cozy womb, and allowed myself to fall apart.

I cried about the sappy storylines, the veteran drag queens eliminated unceremoniously on the first episode for being boring, the produced-to-death conversations between cast members about trouble finding love, the zero-stakes drama—because most contestants would go on to be famous whether they won or not. I cried on episode 5 of *All Stars* Season 1, when best friends Raven and Jujubee were forced to lip-sync against each other to survive, the two alternating between sobbing and gasping for air for the entire length of Robyn's "Dancing on My Own." I cried at every makeup challenge that ended with a straight woman staring into the mirror, in awe of what a gay man had done to her face. And when I finished crying, that was that. I was finished crying. This strategy worked for a long time.

Until it didn't. The shooting impacted everyone and everything I knew. I could not keep my eyes open without being confronted by memorabilia, could not close them without seeing shattered cocktail glasses. At the movies, another man with a gun might be lurking by the emergency exit. With friends, every conversation ended with someone excusing themselves to go to the bathroom and returning red-eyed with desperate smiles plastered on their faces. I don't know how other queer people manage to go out into a world where we are thrown into the streets by our loved ones, damned to hell by our spiritual leaders, beaten, taunted, and killed, but my way worked. Don't think about or look at it. Don't worry. It worked until that became impossible.

In those first few weeks, because I couldn't avert my attention, I found something else to occupy it. Omar Mateen stepped into Pulse to scare us, so every night I went to Parliament House to prove how unafraid I was. I said I was proud. I said, along with everyone else, *We can't let them scare us into hiding. We can't let him kill us too.*

It felt political to support our businesses, especially now that Pulse was a campaign tool. Every whiskey sour was activism. Every vodka soda a brick thrown in our defense. And while the news outlets updated the list of victims, the bar was the only place where we could go see who survived. My best friends were all safe. The people I was looking for were the ones I'd danced with whose names I didn't know. The punk kid with the green Mohawk who gave me bad Molly one New Year's. The leathery woman with the faded Tinker Bell tramp stamp who always tipped queens by tucking singles into their bras. Where were they? How many people do you know like that? People whose hair you've held back, who you buy your coffee from, people who, if they disappeared, you wouldn't have any way of reaching? Each drink gave me a few more minutes to search. To hope I'd get the chance to say Arturo's words: *Thank God, you weren't there.* Yet even when I did, all I could picture were the people who had been.

Like a man I'd met at Savoy, where the bartender kept a gun above the register just in case. I was around twenty-two at the time; he, a few years older and sitting alone. I'd liked his spiky black hair, the spider webs of laugh lines cracking his cheeks, and so I sidled up next to him and hoped he'd notice. He smiled, bought me a lemon shot. When we kissed, his lips were sweet and sticky with cocktail syrup. I don't remember my exact age, but I remember that. I remembered that years later, when the woman at the yard sale asked if I knew anyone who died. "No," I said. "I didn't know anyone." That night, I drank to finding the Mohawk. The next, I drank to being alive. All month, I drank. To showing my support. Because drinks were free. Because I'd already had two. Because life sucked when I wasn't drunk, and at least when I was, I didn't have to think. About the queer people trying to donate blood to victims being turned away from blood banks because the law assumes we all have AIDS. About the cell phones a woman at a vigil told me rang inside the club for days. About whether the man from Savoy would still be alive if we'd kept in touch.

I drank so much I woke up one morning sprawled out in the back seat of my car, vomit drying on my shirt. I was parked miles away from the club printed on my wristband. I didn't feel guilty about drunk driving, though it was beyond stupid and selfish. I took myself home, fell into bed, swallowed a Valium. I watched *RuPaul's Drag Race*, not feeling much of anything.

That's where I was the night an ad for California sprang up on YouTube. In my numbness, the images on-screen seemed brighter than they were, tinted with destiny. Kim Kardashian brushed up on quantum physics by the pool. Betty White zipped around a film set on a golf cart. Since then I've realized it must have been a targeted ad from the endless hours I'd spent applying to a graduate writing program in SoCal almost a full year before. After not hearing back for months, I'd assumed I didn't make the cut. At some point I got a call informing me I did. Though I accepted the invitation, I never seriously believed I would go. It would be too expensive to move. I had no savings. No people out there. The last time I tried to leave home I came crawling back less than six months later. I only applied because I wanted to have proof that in another life, one where I had the money to chase my dreams, I would have been important.

"Get out here!" Betty White said now, and what I heard was: Another life? Oh, shut up. You still have this one, idiot! Use it!

She was right. All the practical reasons I couldn't go felt insignificant considering that if I stayed and continued in the direction I was headed, I would end up dead or strangling the owner of any dog I saw in a Bark 4 Pulse onesie. So why not try? Why not start over? Out there I could be the kind of person who spent their days tending to a succulent garden with a big floppy hat on, drinking kombucha from a mason jar. I could walk along the beach in white linen pants and dip my toes into the Pacific Ocean. What did I have to lose? Orlando was so small, and California was so big and far away.

When the pilot announced we were flying over Los Angeles, I raised my shade and watched the city unroll beneath me in intricate gray grids, like a faded Persian rug. Already I felt like a new person, including the one I told the program coordinator I was over email: someone with years of education and publishing experience, someone important. It wasn't lying. It was drag. She'd offered me a position teaching undergraduates writing, a job typically reserved for second- and third-year students. The passengers clapped politely as the plane dipped to give us a clearer view. Twenty minutes later, when we touched ground at our destination, Riverside, where I'd be living, they clapped again, because things could only get better.

In those early weeks in California, with no car to drive to the beach in and little money for artisanal probiotics, I spent most of my time exploring my new zip code on foot. Riverside. It was such an idyllic name. A side of river to go with my new, gentle existence. And walking around, I couldn't get over how much the city resembled a Bob Ross painting. Not one of his finished paintings of quaint landscapes with names that sound like Yankee Candle scents—*The Old Mill*, *Light House at Night*—but those at the stage where he's just getting things started and guides his audience to take a slop of color and smudge it across their canvases, leaving them scratching their heads and wondering what the hell they'd gotten themselves into.

Girl, it was a desert. A scorched, dusty desert.

Each morning, I prayed a hand would descend from the smog clouds and fill in all the parts of California Betty White promised: add trees to the bone-dry mountains, transform the heroin needles scattered at the bus stop into darling pinecones. No one I asked in the program knew anything about a river, and even if I had a car, with traffic L.A. was two whole hours away. Riverside's closest connection to

Hollywood was that *Breaking Bad* was originally set to take place there. In the nineties, it was considered the meth capital of the world.

I discovered this when I googled the city, days after arriving, something I admittedly should have thought to do before. Perhaps, I don't know, when I bought my one-way plane ticket. In the whirlwind of wanting to get away from Orlando, I'd only investigated where I was going enough to find a place to live. Now that I'd signed a two-year lease, I added "gay" to my search. An article popped up in my results that ranked Riverside the third most homophobic city in the country, based on a study that analyzed the frequency of derogatory tweets. A friend suggested that maybe there was just one really homophobic guy tweeting "die faggots" a thousand times a day, skewing the results. That might have reassured me if I didn't know all too well what one really homophobic person is capable of.

Still, I tried to push my anxiety aside. No matter how disappointing Riverside was, at least there was a gay bar. It had a cool name too. The Menagerie. Another Google search revealed that in 2002 it was the site of a hate crime involving a gang of skinheads who stabbed and killed a man and injured another, screaming, "You want some trouble . . . fag, here it is!" At that point I decided to stop googling.

On a night when I finished grading my students' stories early, I squeezed into a pair of tight jeans and invited a classmate, Ava, and her friend Vanessa to go with me. Only a few people were scattered around the small, horseshoe-shaped bar when we arrived. A neon sign spelling out the word *fab-ulous* with an *a* ("Fabulaus") hung over the stage. I walked past it to the dance floor, where the walls were paneled with floor-to-ceiling mirrors, and stepped close enough to one to get a good look at my reflection. All my time outdoors had deepened my foundation shade from Rich Tan to Golden. My ass had gotten a little perkier too. These felt like signs from the universe, its way of telling me to stop being a snob. Riverside wasn't that bad. Maybe it only seemed so because it was 2016 and everything else in the world was terrible.

While Ava and Vanessa made friends with some girls at the bar, I danced with the first man who asked. To Mariah. To Madonna. He pulled me in and did that thing guys do where they look at your lips and your eyes and your lips and your eyes. Watching him get closer and closer, my heartbeat accelerated. How long had it been? Three months? Four? Since the boy I'd kissed was shot. A few feet away, another one of us was stabbed to death. No, I said to those thoughts. Not now. I ran over to Ava and Vanessa. Ordered us a round of Jell-O shots, of neon blue drinks. We drank. To have fun. Because Whitney was on. Because I wanted to dance with somebody. Back under the disco lights, my mind quieted down. I threw my hands up, bent low, shook my new, improved ass, sweat dripping down my neck. For a moment nothing was serious. I was someone capable of having fun.

After a few songs Ava and I went outside for fresh air. As the cool night breeze caressed our glistening faces, we stood there smiling, just smiling and breathing.

Then we turned to head back in, and the bouncer held his palm up to my chest.

"You can't come in," he said. His arms were covered with tattoos. Skulls. A Native American chief smoking a blunt. Straight, I guessed.

I thought he was kidding and walked around him. He put his other palm up.

"Seriously," he repeated. "You can't come in."

"What? Why not?" I asked, stepping away.

"The bartender said you've caused trouble here before."

I took out my Florida ID. "I think you're confusing me with someone else," I said, showing it to him and raising my eyebrow at Ava, who shrugged in return. "I just moved here."

"I'm just following orders," he responded.

"I didn't do anything," I said. "I swear. Get the bartender. He'll tell you."

He stared through me, saying nothing.

Pressure built up in my chest. Do not make a scene, I told myself. Be cool. Relax.

"For real, you're not gonna let me in?" I tried one last time, replaying the night in my mind. We'd danced a little, spent good money, didn't bother anyone. He had to be joking.

But he kept on staring at the road like he couldn't hear me.

"Nuh-uh. No. Hell no," I snapped, and before I could stop them, there were tears spilling down my cheeks, every emotion I kept back for the last few months desperate for a release. "Who the fuck do you think you are? Why can't I go in? How fucking dare *you*, some straight dude, tell *me* I can't go into a gay bar. This is bullshit. Look at me! Stop acting like you can't hear me. What the fuck is wrong with you? You don't get to take this away. Not for no reason. If you knew how crazy this is . . . after . . . after . . . No. I just want to be with my friends. Why are you smiling? Why is this funny? Tell me what I did. What did I do? I'll leave, but you have to tell me what the fuck I did."

"I don't make the rules," the bouncer said.

"I'm not whoever you think I am!" I screamed. "You don't know me!"

Through the front entrance, the soft din of house music poured out onto the sidewalk. Two women stumbled out of the bar next door and sat on the curb. They glanced toward us and away. Giggled into each other's shoulders. I'd been them before. Watching some drunk queen doing way too much at a bar. I would have laughed at me too.

I lowered my voice. "Just tell me what I did. That's it."

Eventually the bartender was summoned to identify me. He stormed out, rolling his eyes as he wiped his hands with a white rag. "All right, where is he?" he asked.

"What do you mean?" the bouncer replied, nodding at me. "Right there."

"No," the bartender said. "I told you the guy has short hair."

Ava and I shared a look. I wondered what the rest of the description had been.

"See?" I jumped up and down, vindicated. "I told you!"

The bartender gave me a once-over, then turned to the bouncer. "But if this one is being sassy," he said, "you don't have to let him in either."

I stopped jumping.

"Yeah," the bouncer said. "He's being sassy."

Ava grabbed my arm. "Forget them," she said. "Let's just go." So we did.

Over the next few weeks, no matter what I tried to distract myself with, Pulse found a way to sneak in.

Every date I went on became a Q&A as soon as I told the person I was from Orlando. Every time I sat down to write, it felt like the only subject that wasn't silly or frivolous.

After that night at the Menagerie, I couldn't even mask what was obviously a budding drinking problem with so-called pride anymore. Maybe that was for the best. I applied for a medical marijuana license, figuring weed was at least softer than alcohol.

At my appointment the doctor asked what symptoms I was hoping to treat.

"Post-traumatic stress disorder," I told him, though I wasn't sure if not being able to enter a room without formulating an escape plan counted.

"Were you in the army?" he asked.

I answered no.

"Then from what?"

I worried if I told him the truth, he'd say I was being dramatic. I wasn't there. It wasn't *war*. I should be over it.

"Never mind," I replied. "I meant carpal tunnel. My wrist hurts from typing."

He signed my prescription without further questions.

I don't know what I would have done if he hadn't. Smoking alone in bed watching *RuPaul's Drag Race* was the only thing that didn't feel terrible. It was so mindless, so easy to take in, so delightfully *sassy*. I held my joint up with my limp wrist and melted into my mattress.

One night I was watching old lip-sync videos on YouTube and stumbled upon the keynote address RuPaul gave at his inaugural DragCon, an annual convention that draws drag devotees from all over the world to the Los Angeles Convention Center. Aside from getting to meet your favorite *Drag Race* girls, there are panels on everything from tucking and wig styling to drag as a form of activism. But according to him, DragCon was even more than that.

"Finding your tribe," RuPaul said, pacing back and forth in front of a rapt audience of thousands, "finding your constituency and your comrades—*that's* what this event is all about. This is a convention of people who understand how important it is to be yourself."

If he'd been barefoot with a beard, I might have dismissed his speech as the ramblings of a cult leader. But RuPaul wore the impeccable, tailored suit of someone who had their life together, so I listened, and beneath his words what I heard was *Pulse is a crime scene. There are skinheads where you live, Nazis in the White House. Gay people are being rounded up in*

Chechnya and sent to death camps. Come here. Forget all that noise. Find your comrades.

What do you have to lose?

The auditorium where the first of the day's scheduled panels was set to take place was crowded when I arrived. By luck I managed to find a seat next to two women who appeared to be in their early thirties. The one closest to me wore blue lipstick that clashed against her pale white skin. She fit in perfectly with all the other attendees who'd broken out their most colorful outfits for the convention, including me in my novelty cat-print T-shirt with 3-D yarn whiskers. Her friend, on the other hand, looked like a high school chaperone in blue jeans and sandals.

As I inspected the pair, I felt like the orphaned baby bird searching for its family in the children's book *Are You My Mother?*

Are *you* my people?

The woman with blue lips noticed my staring.

"Hi, I'm Elaine," she said. "So, you like *Drag Race?*"

"I love it," I told her.

"So do we." Elaine leaned her head on her friend's chest. "This is Pam." After a pause, she pouted and added, "Pam hasn't been herself lately. Have you, girl?"

"Guess I haven't," Pam said, peeling Elaine off her.

I looked around the auditorium. I wasn't sure if this observation was meant for me. I'd only met them a second earlier. Elaine could have said Pam had just escaped a women's prison in Taiwan where she'd been locked up for smuggling ayahuasca through a slit in her armpit and I would have smiled politely and asked if she'd made any friends. I swallowed one of the pot gummy bears I'd brought with me and hoped whatever this was would end quickly.

Elaine took my uncomfortable nod as a cue to continue. "Breakup," she said.

Apparently, after being married for twelve years, one afternoon Pam found condoms in her husband's jeans. That wouldn't have been strange, except she was on the pill. They didn't use condoms. Distraught, she called Elaine for support. Come to California, Elaine said. With her friend's encouragement, Pam booked a flight. She planned on confronting her husband when she returned, but she wanted to take some time to clear her head first, figure out what to say. Elaine thought going to DragCon might cheer her up.

So, yes, Pam hadn't been feeling herself lately. Her husband was almost definitely cheating on her, and her best friend was now spilling her business to a random gay guy like this was *Queer Eye* and I would twirl a wand and repair her marriage.

"Whoa," I said, then swallowed another gummy.

I didn't have any sage advice. If I were her, I would have probably pretended I didn't find the condoms, or had my own affair, or moved.

"Who do you want to win?" I asked, trying to switch to more pleasant conversation. We talked a little about their favorite, Valentina. Before I got the chance to tell them she was also mine, a drag queen in a white latex jumpsuit appeared in front of us. She held the hand of an Asian girl who peeked at me from behind a fan with the word *Shade* printed on it in gold.

"Biiitch," the drag queen said, eyes widening at the empty seats next to me. "Those taken?"

I told her no, and the pair shuffled in sideways.

"You're here alone?" Elaine asked. She looked thrown.

Yes.

"I thought . . . So, you're not waiting for friends?"

No.

"Oh."

I could see the two of them retreating: This kid came here by himself? What did he do to not have anyone? Why is he eating so much candy?

By the time Katya and Trixie Mattel, the hosts of the panel, took their seats onstage, my fingertips hit the bottom of the bag of gummies. I peeked inside, trying not to panic as I multiplied how many I'd eaten by the amount of THC each contained (too many × yikes), while in front of us Trixie launched into her impression of RuPaul doing endless corporate sponsorships: "I think we should take a second to talk about Squarespace." "But first," Katya chimed in, "I've been meaning to tell you all week about these new sheets I got, these Boll & Branch sheets . . ."

They were spot-on. Sometimes the show felt more like an infomercial than, as RuPaul has put it, "a place to showcase the indomitability of the human spirit," whatever that means. I loved RuPaul, but did he really believe I'd find my comrades here, or was he just trying to sell me a T-shirt? I slunk down low in my seat, feeling like an idiot, and popped one last gummy.

Pam and Elaine vanished in the chaos that ensued after the panel ended and hundreds of people attempted to leave through the room's rear doors. As I fumbled toward the exit, shaking, unsteady, I realized, Oh my God, you are the most stoned anyone has ever been. Do not make a scene, I told myself. Be cool. Relax.

Ten minutes later I found myself blinking back tears and staring up at a bunch of mannequins strung up from the ceiling. It was RuPaul's gown exhibit. Each mannequin wore a piece of couture he made famous on the runway during the last nine seasons of *Drag Race*. One featured an iridescent purple gown covered in sequins as delicate as fish scales. Another had its left leg reeled back like it was stuck in limbo between falling and righting herself.

They were beautiful, and I couldn't stop sobbing.

Not because they were beautiful, nor for any metaphorical reason. In fact, the weed planted me firmly in reality. I was hyperaware of the drag queen a few feet away adjusting her chicken cutlets before a photo op, the little girl in a tutu yanking her mother from gown to gown. Everywhere I turned there was someone smiling.

It was, it hit me, the first time I'd been surrounded by happy queer people, in a place where nothing bad had happened, since the attack.

Standing there, I thought, Even after all we've lost, look at us. And suddenly I was twenty-one again, at Pulse to watch the finale of Season 5 of *RuPaul's Drag Race*, sitting cross-legged on the dance floor like it was my living room.

The show is playing on a projection screen onstage, the captions on because no one can go more than two seconds without screaming in tongues: "Yass mawma werk mawma slayyyyy!" We're people who have nothing better to do on a Friday night: The shot boy in a jockstrap hawking test tubes of tequila who frequently messages me on Grindr at three in the morning to ask, *What's up?* Arturo, sipping a whiskey sour and fanning himself with a coaster. Me, in patent leather boots, a daisy in my hair. We don't speak about our blood families, our shitty day jobs. Tonight is for celebrating. Pulse is Roxxxy Andrews's home club, where she performs every weekend, and she's made the top three. She's not going to win though. "Cause she's such a bitch," someone behind me says. "Since when are drag queens supposed to be *nice*?" "Do you want a shot? Two dollars, baby." "Wasn't someone ordering a pizza?" "It's on the table in the back." "Nah, it's the edit. She's ai'ight. She took a picture with me at Forever 21." "Su mama la dejo en una parada de bus. Que perra." "Greyhound? Her mom left her at the Greyhound—" "¿La de Semoran, verdad?" "Yeah, yeah, Alaska's, she's, yeah, she's, yeah . . ." We watch *RuPaul's Drag Race*, cheer when Jinkx Monsoon, Seattle's premiere Jewish narcoleptic drag queen, is crowned, then dance all night to RuPaul music. We are so young and safe and think it will always be this way.

"Are you okay?" a DragCon employee asked. He wore a bright-pink staff shirt and a frown. Behind him, a mannequin in a silver gown hung in the air. The dress had soft, blossom-shaped panels along the bottom half and splintered off into sharp daggers above the waist. It looked like an origami pineapple.

I swiped a tear on my lip with my tongue. The truth: it tasted amazing. If only I could feel this way forever, then I would have an infinite supply to feed on.

"I'm just lost," I answered, praying it was a good-enough lie that he wouldn't make me leave. I opened my guidebook to a map of the convention center. The cavernous, 720,000-square-foot space was divided by aisles named after puns from the show. I knew exactly where I was, but I bit my lip and put on my best damsel-in-distress voice.

"If we're on Realness Road? What's the fastest way to get to Back Rolls Boulevard? I'm late for a panel?"

He told me to go straight down Sickening Street and make a left when I hit the wall of wigs. Glamazon Lane would have been faster, but I followed his directions anyway.

I made it to the intersection of Death Drop Alley and Sissy That Walkway before turning around to make sure the employee wasn't trailing me.

That's when I saw him. An actor. Seated at a booth with a small stack of DVDs. I recognized his face from one of my favorite movies when I was in high school. It was a film about teenagers, and cliques, and breaking free from them. You've seen it. You would have moseyed around his table trying to catch a better look. It'd been years, and I hadn't heard of him landing any major roles since. He had dark bags under his eyes and a patchy beard that gave him the appearance of a man twice his age. I wondered if he'd sold any of his DVDs. Who even bought DVDs anymore? Seated behind those ancient artifacts, he was a relic selling relics.

Other convention goers recognized him too. They whispered among themselves, took one look at his prices, and moved on. A couple of Sharpies lay uncapped by his elbows. He spoke into his cell phone.

"It's going great," I heard him say.

Jesus, was that what I looked like? To the employee? To everyone I told I was okay? Well, damn, fine, maybe nothing was going great. So there. So now what?

I bought pizza. My cell phone died. I was too stoned for any of this.

There was an open power outlet by the bathrooms. I sat down on the floor to charge next to a group of teenage girls wearing neon tinsel wigs. One of them dumped out her tote bag, unleashing an avalanche of condoms and party-sized packages of lube she'd collected at the several sex-education booths throughout the convention center. Pleased with her day's catch, she swept the goodies between her legs and counted each one out loud as she deposited them back into

her bag. It sounded like counting sheep, and around her fif-
tieth, I passed out.

Meanwhile, as I slept, there were hundreds of people standing on a long pink carpet, unrolled just for this occasion. At
the end of the line, all the way over there—Can you see? No,
further back. Behind that partition—was the person they
were all waiting hours to talk to.

Picture him, her, either/or, RuPaul doesn't have a preference. Sitting on a chair? I wouldn't dream of it. A throne!
Gilded, with red velvet cushions. It's RuPaul's meet-and-
greet booth. And what is RuPaul wearing? I don't know. I
was asleep, cradling a half-eaten pizza on a paper plate, tears
drying on my cheeks, a teenage girl looking at me like What
happened to him? Yikes. Back to her loot. Fifty-one condoms. Fifty-three. Sixty.

The line inched forward. Was it a minute? Was it even
that? How much time do you get with RuPaul? Also, what
do you say? What can you possibly say to God?

You could start with *I love the show.*

Thank you, RuPaul would answer, while the professional
photographer arranges you next to him. He doesn't want you
to take a selfie. It's not personal. RuPaul is asked for selfies
every day, and when the picture is too close, or the angle
is all wrong, he is asked for another and another until it is
perfect. He wants it to be perfect the first time. He has a life
to live, damn.

So be quick: Big fan of your work. You look fantastic. I

just want you to know that when *Drag Race* is on, I forget people hate us, that my husband cheated on me, what got taken away.

Thank you, thank you, thank you, he answers. Really. He means it. To prove it to you, here it is with furrowed brows, with a sage nod, with a sigh, stamped forever in a perfect picture: *Thank you.*

And even if it was all bullshit it would be wonderful. Worth any price. I think it would have been. I don't know. Because while other people were meeting RuPaul, my pizza was sliding off the edge of my plate, leaving a grease stain on my jeans that would remind me for weeks that instead of meeting God, I got stoned and fell asleep on the floor.

There's this video I watch when I want to get in my feelings. It stars a *Drag Race* girl before she made it on the show. Valentina. Pam's favorite, and mine. She's onstage at a packed bar in West Hollywood, wearing a white wedding dress cinched to within an inch of its life, her hair pulled back into a black bun adorned with orchids. Diamonds hang from her ears, winking in the spotlight as she lip-syncs to Isabel Pantoja's "Así Fue."

Written by Juan Gabriel, the lyrics are about a woman whose lover has abandoned her. No warning, no last words. She wakes up one morning and finds he is simply gone. Devastated, she cries like she's never cried before. It seems like she'll never get over her heartbreak, but over time, she somehow manages to. The earth does another spin. She falls in love with another man. But of course, right when she's found happiness, out of nowhere, the woman's old lover returns and expects them to pick up where they'd left off. There's anger and fear in Valentina's eyes as she lip-syncs to Isabel's frazzled, bitter voice. She's sorry, Isabel sings, but what does he want from her? Was her life supposed to stop while he was away? He can't possibly blame her for moving on. Good luck, she tells him. You will not hurt me again.

In contrast to the somber lyrics, the audience is delighted, their faces rapt. Valentina makes the singer's pain seem almost glamorous. Her movements are small yet fierce. Dollar bills shower her as her hands dance through the air, grazing her chest, framing her face, slinking down her curves. She struts up and down the stage like it's her personal catwalk. She is so deep into the fantasy she barely notices the people throwing fistfuls of cash at her feet.

It's chaotic, this performance of grief. The sparkling wedding gown. The over-the-top mixture of anguish and sexiness. It's peak drag: painful, messy, a constant negotiation between holding in and spilling out. Aside from the tucking, there's corsetry digging into your ribs, padding suffocating your skin, wig tape pulling at your skull, feet stuffed and forced into unnatural angles. It's uncomfortable, and still people want more. They want you to bear it and look beautiful, to know the words.

But I don't. I don't know the word for what it felt like to wake up at DragCon and realize I was wasting my life trying to change it. The word for those moments when I remember what people want to do to us and I want to unzip my skin suit and walk into a fire, be a faggot on my own terms. I wish I knew a word that would wash all the *Thank God you weren't theres* out of my mouth, another for what I would give to be able to say them forty-nine more times. If I knew the words for these things, I would string them all together over a bed of violins. I would be like Valentina, hope it's enough to move my lips, bear my hurt. I'm tired. Let someone else sing.

High-Risk Homosexual

Dr. Chen got highlights.

When I'd first met her at my college health center, she had a blunt, jet-black bob that complemented her trim, athletic figure. It was the perfect aerodynamic haircut for someone who wanted to get their work done and leave the room fast, which was exactly what I'd wanted too.

Back then our consultations had the no-nonsense air of a trial. I presented my case—I am a gay man who would like to have some gay sex—and she filled out the necessary paperwork to make that happen. She did not ask why. She did not even think it, because the character of her in my mind had no thoughts. She was no more sentient than a webpage.

But now, after a month of appointments during which I'd told her more about who I'd slept with than I had my closest friends, there were chunky streaks in her hair that could aptly be described as *honey*. I wasn't unreasonable. It wasn't that I didn't want Dr. Chen looking cute. It was just that what we were doing here was easier when I could pretend she was above such trivial, human concerns as highlights. If she had thoughts about her appearance, it meant she was capable of having thoughts about other things, like her patients. Did she think me and my gay sex were disgusting, or weird, or funny? Who was she if not a webpage that couldn't judge me?

"I've been having nightmares," I told her.

She typed this into a form on her computer, then adjusted her rolling chair so that her feet brushed back and forth over the ground. I recognized her shoes. I'd sold hundreds of them at the flip-flop boutique where I worked before grad school. They were white espadrilles with yellow polka dots, made by one of those companies that promise that with each purchase, a pair will be donated to an orphan somewhere hot with hard, clay earth. My chest felt lighter. She cared about orphans. She probably was a normal amount of homophobic. Fifteen percent. She'd cry if one of her kids came out to her, but in her room.

"Nightmares," she repeated.

"Yeah. Almost every night for the last two weeks."

One of her eyebrows went up. The movement looked rehearsed, like a trick she'd learned in medical school meant to convey the proper level of concern. Everything about this visit had a trace of acting to it. I requested a drug I didn't technically need. She responded by reading questions off a script. "Do you prefer to give or receive?" she'd asked during my last visit, as if the question weren't about anal but my philosophy on Christmas.

She sighed and turned to her computer, presumably to check whether nightmares were a symptom of the medication she'd prescribed me. Privately I scolded myself for bringing them up. They weren't supposed to become A Thing, not when my being here was already A Thing.

I was one of her first patients on Truvada, commonly known as PrEP, the one-a-day antiviral pill that has been shown to reduce your risk of HIV infection by nearly 100 percent. As of 2017, it had been used for over a decade by HIV-positive people to treat the virus, but it wasn't until 2012 that the FDA approved it for use by those who are HIV-negative as a means of prevention. Even though PrEP had been available for five years by the time I met Dr. Chen, the drug's manufacturer reported that between 2012 and 2014, only 3,253 people started the PrEP regimen. It was expensive ($1,300 a month without health insurance), and so new, so risky. It wasn't clear what an antiretroviral medication would do to an HIV-negative body. It still isn't.

Which was why I needed to be the perfect gay male specimen for Dr. Chen. If I showed too many negative side effects, I worried she would hesitate before prescribing PrEP to other queer people. I had forgotten there were times when I spoke for myself and times when I spoke on behalf of all gay men. I wouldn't slip up again.

"It's not a big deal," I told her. "I googled it. Aren't nightmares common for the first few weeks?" I knew they were.

I'd assumed she did as well, considering she'd prescribed the drug to me. The nightmares weren't that bad anyway. In my last one, Mariah Carey tried to eat me with an ice cream scooper. I kind of looked forward to them.

"Yes, you're right. Nightmares are normal," Dr. Chen said, reading from her screen. She went through the list of other symptoms I might expect: Fever. Headache. Vomiting and diarrhea.

"Night sweats, sore throat, tiredness," I added. "I feel fine."

None of these bothered me when I researched PrEP on my own. I didn't care if the pills made me projectile vomit diarrhea out of my sore throat. Soon I would be able to date without worrying about the virus that decimated the generation of queer people who came before me. As long as I could find someone who didn't mind my incontinent mouth, it'd be worth it.

"It sounds like you know what you're doing," Dr. Chen said, rolling away from her computer. We began our recap.

"How many partners have you had in the past month?" she asked.

A poster on the wall listed the effectiveness of various birth contraceptives, ranking them with gold stars. Condoms, male or female: one gold star. Diaphragms: three gold stars. Pulling out: no gold stars. A crude drawing of a hand with crossed fingers represented just how few stars the pulling-out method deserved.

"Like, boyfriends? Or intercourse?" I don't know why I

asked for the clarification. The answer would have been the same either way. None. I hadn't had sex in months.

"Intercourse," she said. "How many partners have you slept with in the last couple of weeks?"

I hesitated. If I answered none, would she think I didn't need PrEP and take me off the medication entirely? I hadn't been sexually active *lately*, but what if I met someone? Would a condom be enough to protect me? The poster in the room said it was a one-star contraceptive.

"Two partners," I blurted out, figuring that was better than nothing.

She wrote the number in my chart.

"Did you use protection?"

"Yes," I answered.

"And did you pay either of them money in exchange for sex?"

"No."

"Okay." She took a deep breath and giggled as if she were about to ask for my autograph. "I'm sorry, but I have to ask. You didn't meet either of your partners online or anything, right?"

"No," I said again.

She lowered her pen to my chart once more, muttering "Didn't meet partners online" under her breath, then added, "Good, good."

All of this was standard protocol. Part of the agreement we made that I would meet with her every few weeks to recount my latest sexual activity and check for liver damage—a potential side-effect of the drug. It took two weeks for the antiviral to reach a high-enough level to fight HIV, and about two more for the nausea and nightmares to disappear. With my first month behind me, it was time for her to hold up her end of the bargain—another bottle of PrEP.

"You doing all right?" she asked.

"I'm doing all right," I told her.

I would be, once she handed me my permission slip to go off and have fearless sex. We sat quietly as my prescription printed line by line.

Before I could read what was on it, she folded the paper in half and pressed it into my palm. It wasn't until I made it home twenty minutes later that I opened it. My first thought was that there'd been a mistake, that I'd gotten someone else's diagnosis.

Dispense to Edgar Gomez
Twenty-Five Years Old
High-Risk Homosexual

There was my name. That was my age. But "high-risk homosexual"?

Girl, where?

According to the fake sexual history I'd given her, I'd slept with just two men in a whole month. Men I'd supposedly met in person, not in seedy parks or truck-stop bathroom stalls or wherever else "risky" people hooked up. I didn't pay. I used imaginary condoms and everything.

What about any of that made me a high-risk homosexual?
I dug through my desk drawers looking for my original
prescription. There I found myself again, buried under loose
paper clips. Edgar Gomez. High-risk homosexual. So there
wasn't a mistake. She meant it. How hadn't I noticed that
before? I must have been so thrilled to qualify for PrEP on
my initial consult that I didn't bother to read the fine print.

Sitting alone in my bedroom, suddenly I felt exactly as I
did in high school the day that I went to my guidance counselor's office to discuss college. I'd gone into the meeting figuring we'd talk about my strong SAT scores or the several
college-level courses I'd taken. We did briefly, but then the
conversation turned to financial aid, and my counselor began
listing all the different scholarships available to me: for being
gay, for being the first generation in my family to be born in
the United States, for living in a single-parent household. I
was grateful there was money out there, but I couldn't help
resenting what I believed I had to do to accept it, which was
to take those things I'd slowly begun to take pride in—my
queerness, my family's migration—and claim they'd put me
at a disadvantage. In many ways they did, but I wasn't ready
to admit that. It seemed cruel, after all the work I'd put into
loving myself, that the final step left between me and going
to college was writing several five-hundred-word personal
essays about how much my life sucked.

Though I hated being reduced to a narrative of victim-
hood, my counselor wasn't wrong to assume I needed help.
The truth was that I couldn't have afforded to go without aid,

so I put my pride aside and applied. And it was this same truth that I was learning again years later: my story wasn't just mine; who I was resided somewhere between how I saw myself and how everyone else—my counselor, the organizers of those scholarships, Dr. Chen—did.

No, I didn't think I was high-risk, yet at the same time: Could I afford to say I wasn't?

The week before my visit with Dr. Chen, when I was still waiting for the PrEP to kick in, a man traveling on business messaged me on Grindr, inviting me to his hotel room. I've always been jealous of my gay friends who hook up with abandon. The ones who visit bathhouses as casually as if they were going candle shopping at Target. The apps allow me to pretend I'm like them. Chill about sex. Reading the man's message, I tried to picture myself showing up to his room. The door would be unlocked, he told me. He'd be waiting inside, facedown, ass up on the mattress. I could do whatever I wanted. I began to type out a response, but then the same anxiety crept in that always did, instantly shattering my desire.

What if I brushed my teeth too hard, and in one of the back rows there was a little cut, small enough not to notice but big enough for HIV to wiggle its way in?

My nails. I bite them till they bleed. All those wounds. What if his semen touches my fingers and . . . ?

And if the condom slips off? Or breaks? And if he bites my lip? And if he doesn't regularly get tested?

I logged out. It was too . . . stressful. Too . . . scary. The rare times I did have casual sex, I had to bury my face in a pillow to stifle my nervous laughter while thinking, Hope he's worth it, because this might kill you!

It wasn't funny, but it felt true.

Perhaps educating myself would have relieved my overblown fear, but the little I did know about HIV terrified me enough, and I was afraid of what else I might discover if I looked closer. I knew the stigma surrounding HIV was so pervasive that even for people who are positive and undetectable (meaning the amount of virus in their blood is so low it is virtually impossible to transmit), dating became more difficult than it already was. The language men use on the apps alone was proof of that: "Clean and looking for same," some write, like having an STD makes you *dirty*. I knew that in high school Miguel had been cautious of sharing his status with me to the point that he constantly accused strangers of having AIDS, probably to gauge my reaction before deciding whether I was trustworthy. I knew there was medicine, he must have been on it, but that it was costly, and in a year the insurance I had through grad school would end. Add to all that what I knew from television and films.

If my life was to be anything like those of the queer people on Lifetime, after coming out of the closet as a teenager, I was destined to spend the next few years dodging mobs of gay bashers. College would be a montage of close-ups of me inhaling poppers under a disco light, pairs of underwear strewn on my bedroom floor next to empty bottles of vodka.

These would be the "fun" years, artfully selected to seduce viewers into thinking the gay lifestyle was worth it. But then, some distant morning at the wise gay age of twenty-seven, I would wake up with a sharp pain in my thigh, trace it with my fingertips to a purple lesion. A few months later a nurse would be spoon-feeding me applesauce at a hospice. Flash forward to my funeral, my mother draped over my casket, one or two friends in the back of the church. The ending credits would roll over the image of them weeping, the survivors, left behind to warn the next generation.

That last part, at least, isn't fiction, because the gay people who lived through the crisis *did* warn me. In the art I grew up with. In the cautionary tales many of them told. Be careful, they said. Sex can kill you. Look what it did to us. I don't doubt their words came from a place of love and immeasurable hurt. They couldn't have known the side effects of hearing that message over and over, that screenwriters would take it and multiply it by a thousand so straight people would have something morbid and exotic to consume for their entertainment, that I would turn to those movies seeking reflection and find in them only loss. They just wanted me to have a chance. Now there was a new voice saying: With PrEP, you do. Write something new.

After reading Dr. Chen's diagnosis, I logged on to Grindr, fell into bed, and covered my head with a pillow. To go from "If you sleep with someone, you'll die" to "Just kidding! Be a ho!" was such an earth-shattering shift that I still couldn't believe one pill a day was all it took. My phone vibrated with a new message. I poked my head out from beneath my pillow.

His name was Carlos, and he was only free for a few hours. Did I want to join him in his car for some fun?

Within forty-five minutes, I was in the passenger seat of a Mustang, admiring the spaceship features on his dashboard and trying to act casual. This wasn't revolutionary. We weren't exploring alien territory. He and I were just two people, about to fuck.

"You're on PrEP, right?" he asked almost immediately.

"Uh-huh," I said, though I'd already told him so in our messages.

A small monitor below his radio fed footage from a hidden camera in the rear of his car. Behind us, there was nothing but gravel. We were parked in a spot tucked behind my apartment. I didn't want him coming inside. I didn't want my roommates thinking I was the kind of guy who met randos online and brought them home. A high-risk homosexual, or whatever.

"Cool. Wanna move to the back?" He unbuckled his seatbelt. "There's more room."

I kept my eyes on the gravel.

"Don't you want to turn your car off?" I asked.

He crawled over the divider, briefly looking over his shoulder to say, "Nah. This shouldn't take that long."

It didn't.

Half an hour later I was back in bed with my palm resting on my stomach, feeling Carlos swimming inside of me.

I couldn't remember ever being so aware of my body. Then again, I rarely swallowed. I hated the taste of semen, how you couldn't ever predict the flavor, the way some men squeezed out every drop and presented it to me as if it were artisanal toothpaste.

Somewhere in my belly, something growled. The air conditioner rattled away on its coolest setting. A trickle of sweat fell from my forehead, snaking its way down my neck. Is it working? Is it working? Is it working? I wondered, thinking about the miracle drug that was meant to take this anxiety away.

What if you didn't take enough?

Or you needed to wait a little longer for it to become effective? What if you're one of the 0.01 percent it doesn't work on? What if you're exactly who everyone thinks you are?

Dr. Chen was on vacation. Beyond the highlights, now I couldn't help imagining her sipping a mai tai on a Carnival Cruise, flip-flops tapping along to a ukulele cover of a Jimmy Buffett song. We were two months into my treatment. She'd scheduled my monthly checkup and STD screening with a laboratory technician I'd never met.

"How you doing today?" this new woman asked. Her braids were pulled back into a pineapple bun. She hovered over me wearing palm-tree-patterned scrubs. Maybe it was because we were in California, but all the staff at Dr. Chen's office seemed obsessed with the beach. A faux-grass table skirt hung from the reception desk. Dr. Chen's screensaver was of the sun setting behind the ocean. Next to the contraception posters on the wall were framed black-and-white pictures of seashells. I assumed the relentlessly tropical vibe was meant to put patients at ease, their way of forcing us to think happy thoughts. This was mine: I'm a kid, and my mom wants to go to Cocoa Beach—I don't know why. The water there is dirty. There's litter everywhere. At night, cops roam the shore with flashlights to scare away homeless people. She wants to leave the house, she says. She wants to do *something*! We never do *anything*! Probably she chooses Cocoa because it's closest. We blast her favorite Bon Jovi CD on the drive over. Park for free at the surf shop a block away from shore and walk. I see a white sun ahead. Black water. Purple sand. It looks like God ran out of the right crayons.

As we get closer, it becomes clear it's not the sand that's purple. It's jellyfish. There are thousands of them, dead. The tide has swept their corpses in and deposited them all around us. Their soft bodies bake in the heat, reeking of gas-station sushi. Mom, in her yellow sundress, airs out a towel and sets it down in a small space that's clear of corpses, then takes a seat. I follow. From her purse, she extracts a salad and a hamburger we picked up from Wendy's. She does this in silence, working slowly, deliberately, and says just one thing about the graveyard: "Look, jellyfish." I watch her arrange a fork and napkin next to the salad, unwrap the hamburger.

"Which one do you want?" she asks.

I love this game. We play it when she doesn't have enough

money to pay for one of my field trips but lets me cut class to hang out with her at the airport. The game where she affectionately calls the city's discount food pantry "my little place downtown." I grab the hamburger and take a bite as if nothing weird is happening.

"It's my life," she whispers, brushing my shoulder with her knuckle, "it's now na-na-na."

We turn our noses away from the wind when it blows the stink of decay our way.

"I'm fine," I told the technician. There was almost zero chance I'd contracted HIV from Carlos.

She rubbed a cotton ball with alcohol over a spot on my right arm until a vein surfaced. "Got any fun plans this weekend?"

"I'm going to Pride."

"Oh, nice!" she said, and then: "What's that?"

"Gay Pride. It's like a festival. There's a parade in L.A."

A smile spread across her face. "That's so . . . nice." She stepped away, returning a moment later wearing latex gloves. Standard protocol.

I closed my eyes when she punctured the vein with a needle. My blood crawled up through a plastic wire and filled up one, then another vial. Six in total. From there to the lab. Even after getting tested dozens of times, I've never gotten used to the terror that sweeps over me in the minutes before I get my results. I want to be someone who is at peace with what happens next. To remember HIV does not have to be a death sentence anymore. Remember my friends who carry the virus and live full, satisfying lives despite the world telling them they are tragic. It helps, in those moments, to tell myself I have a say in how my story gets told, to stare at the seashells on the walls, see my mom and me sitting down at the beach, unwrapping our lunch.

Look, my pounding heart warned me, she's back.

All clear.

After Carlos, there was Jose. He didn't ask me if I was on PrEP. He didn't ask anything. Our messages could have fit on a napkin. *Hey. Hey back. Come over. Alright.*

I wasn't as tense as usual on the cab ride to Jose's place, now that I was sure the drug worked. The driver pulled into an apartment complex that shared a fence with a grocery store. Jose greeted me by some bushes. When I walked into his room, he flipped the lights off and pulled my pants and briefs down with one ravenous tug. They became a part of his mattress, which was just a bundle of clothes on the floor surrounded by dirty dishes. Sex with him was like tumbling inside of a washing machine. As the two of us caught our breath before another round, something nagged at me. In the rush of excitement, we'd forgotten to use a condom. I knew I was safe—from HIV anyway, PrEP doesn't protect you from any other STD—but judging by the state of his place, I doubted he was on it.

"Are you ever, like, nervous?" I asked, my cheek pressed against his sweaty chest.

He walked two fingers along my arm. "Of what?"

Christian taught music at the city college. There was a guitar-shaped stain on the carpet of his office that I swore was too obvious to be true. He made me promise I'd keep his sneaking me in after hours a secret, as if we had any mutual friends I might tell. When he came, he made a face like I'd gut-punched him.

"You know. STDs. HIV or whatever." I stared up at the pale dent in Jose's nose from wearing glasses. He felt around the floor until he found them, then put them on.

"Why?" he asked, pulling his fingers off my arm. "Do you have it?"

Ben had a memory foam mattress, a bucket of condoms, and a towel sewn onto his pillow. ("I slobber.")

"No," I said. "It's just. We didn't use a . . . We should have. But no, I don't."

Jesus asked me if I liked surprises. The morning after we hooked up, he woke me up with his dick in my mouth. I didn't think that was what he meant.

"Oh," Jose said, his voice growing uneasy. "Then why'd you ask?"

Justin didn't kiss.

"Forget it. I'm stupid," I said. "Anyway, I'm on PrEP."

Andrew did. Everywhere. Ears. Neck. Places I didn't know should be kissed. Just below and to the left of my belly button. The soft spot where my spine met my lower back.

Jose sat up. "What's that?"

Jamal was so loud I think he just wanted to piss off his roommates.

"It's that drug. For HIV? You haven't heard of it?"

Luis asked if he could wear his headphones while we fucked. I thought it was sweet that he was open with his weirdness, even though my gold chain kept getting tangled in his cords.

"Whoa," Jose said. He pulled his shirt back on and stood up. "So you *do* have it?"

"No," I told him. "It's preventative."

David's poppers spilled in the back seat of his car. We tried to finish before the fumes suffocated us but barely lasted a minute. I was too delirious to care whether my roommates heard us scramble into the apartment.

"Right." He went around his room putting things away. "Right. Listen, man, I have work in the morning, so . . ."

Jemmy broke up with his girlfriend after our first time, said he needed to see me every night, come on, please baby, what are you up to, you there? I couldn't date someone that newly out. He had a lot of catching up to do. You're going to want to sleep around, I told him. Trust me.

Most of the men I slept with weren't on PrEP, didn't seem concerned with anything but what we were doing right then. I wanted to know what made them confident. What they knew that I didn't. We'd grown up reading the same news headlines, watching the same after-school specials. Did they think they'd be the exception? Did they just not care? Or were they secretly rich and figured they'd be able to handle whatever happened? After Jose, I understood their attitudes weren't as simple as they first appeared, that these men had their own complicated relationships to sex that they didn't need to disclose to me. Perhaps they were putting on a front of bravery, like I used to. Perhaps they knew anything worth doing contained an element of risk.

I knew so much about that. The risk. But hardly anything about the worth. My ears had been so clogged with fear before that I couldn't possibly enjoy what was happening. With every bed I crawled into, I discovered how much I'd been missing. All this time there were men touching me, licking me, asking a question just as important as "Are you ever, like, nervous?"

When I opened my mouth to answer them, it was all I could do not to laugh. "Yes, that feels good," I said, burying my face into their pillows.

It was funny because it was true. Finally, it felt good.

Three months. Four months. Five. Another liver checkup. Another STD test. Dr. Chen emailed me saying I needed to come in. It was urgent.

A nurse led me to a different room than usual. On this wall, a safe-sex poster compared condom usage to wearing a seatbelt: "Don't ride without one." The wax paper beneath me made a noise like static as I shifted my weight on the examination bed. I crossed my legs and the paper made the noise again. I kept still until I heard a knock on the door. Dr. Chen stepped in without waiting for an answer.

"How've you been?" she asked casually.

"Okay," I said, less frightened than I would have been were I not on PrEP, but confused about why she'd summoned me.

"And how's your body feeling lately?" She scanned the clipboard in her hand and flipped through a few pages.

"Normal," I told her.

"No diarrhea?" she pressed on. "Stomach aches? Abdomen pain?"

"No."

"Nothing at all?"

She didn't believe me. With these lab results, something had to hurt.

"I'm fine," I said again. I had to be.

I wasn't.

My liver. It was showing early signs of failure. Dr. Chen spoke quickly: Elevated bilirubin. Jaundice. Dialysis. What? What? What the *fuck*?

"No, it's not AIDS." She smiled tenderly.

I was having a rare reaction to PrEP. I was young, she said. Brushed my teeth twice a day, took the stairs. PrEP was the only recent change in my life. There was no other explanation. The drug meant to protect me from contracting the deadly virus was, in fact, killing me.

This was what the checkups were for, she reminded me; then she gave me two options.

I could stay on PrEP. We would closely monitor my liver while I continued my high-risk homosexual activity. One morning I might wake up with tea-colored skin, my sheets soaked in piss, but isn't that the reality every person lives with? You are healthy until one day you are not.

The second option was to give the drug up. Go back to my unsatisfying, once-a-year sex, to frantically scouring the internet for symptoms of disease only moments after touching another man. No more fun. Accept defeat. Accept the lesson queer people learned when the AIDS crisis began: We don't get to behave like everyone else. No, it's not fair. Oh well.

"What do you think I should do?" I asked Dr. Chen.

After wanting her to hand me my medicine with no judgment, no thoughts, what I craved most of all now was her opinion. She set her clipboard down.

"Well," she moved closer. "Do you still think you're high-risk?"

"Yes," I said. "I mean, I don't know. I guess. No?"

If we were using the criteria she used to diagnose me when we first met—sex twice a month, with protection, and never with a man I'd met online—then I certainly still was. But I never thought that was risky to begin with. Besides, since then I'd discovered that most new HIV diagnoses in women are attributed to heterosexual sex. I doubted that if I were a straight woman requesting PrEP she would have deemed me a high-risk *heterosexual*. I wanted to keep having good, weird sex. I wanted to stay alive. I wanted, mostly, for no one to ever look at me and feel sorry. Yet if I had been taught HIV is the inevitable fate for so many of us, the worst thing that could possibly happen, wasn't it natural for other people, for her, to think the same thing too?

I didn't know Dr. Chen, not really. I met with her for half an hour once a month and took guesses at the unfilled-in details of her life. I chose her because she had a bob. I thought that meant she was a serious person who did not allow her personal biases to get in the way of her work. And then, one morning, she showed up with highlights.

And what did she know about me? That I was gay, Latinx, in my mid-twenties, sexually active. Adding those together, she arrived at the conclusion that I was a high-risk homosexual.

We were each taking stabs at who the other was, and neither of us was right.

I didn't know what to tell her. I didn't particularly feel high-risk, but given the history of HIV among queers and the disproportionate rates that it affected Latinx people, I couldn't exactly say I wasn't. I was stuck.

"I'm special," I told her. It wasn't an answer to her question. "Like, of all the patients you will ever have, I'm especially weak. One time I fainted after slicing my thumb on a can of tuna at my mom's house. She had to drag me to her bedroom." I left out the part about how relieved I was when I woke up and it hit me she hadn't called an ambulance. Who had that kind of money?

Dr. Chen didn't raise her eyebrow.

"I know that PrEP isn't working for me, but I don't want you think it won't work for anyone else. It's me. I'm just . . . special."

For the first time, I tried to stop thinking of Dr. Chen as who I wanted her to be. Stopped imagining her as my icy sex attorney. Stopped picturing her on a Carnival Cruise. I confessed I was worried she wouldn't prescribe PrEP to others because of me, and then I let her speak for herself.

She admitted she was concerned about PrEP. A patient had recently come in with a strange rash, another with abnormally dry skin that looked like scales.

"PrEP brings strange things out in people," she said. "I don't hand it out like candy."

"Then who do you give it to?" I asked.

She shrugged. "Usually the people who ask for it have a good reason."

That night, I emptied the pills into my toilet, watching them sink to the bottom of the bowl, their blue coating washing off and rising to the water's surface like smoke signals. I flushed, because right then it was more dangerous to keep doing everything to avoid the disease than to learn to live a life that acknowledged it as possible outcome, but only that.

HIV is treatable. It is, I've heard people say, no worse than a cold, when you consider all of the medical advancements that have been made. A very, very expensive cold. Nonfatal, so long as you have insurance. There is medicine, you know. There's PrEP.

Briefly, it allowed me to stare down my fear from a safe distance. Now when I hook up, I don't have the comfort of knowing with statistic certainty the probability that I won't contract HIV. For the uninsured, for those whose bodies reject the drug, in many parts of the world, fear is not irrational. I can't shrug off the prudish, pre-PrEP version of myself and hide him somewhere deep in my closet like a gaudy old outfit I used to adore way back when. Whether the sex is good or bad, I continue to wonder:

What will I do if, or when, I get it?

Will people think I'm one of the *good* ones? Careful? Sexless?

Or that I'm reckless, and I'll sleep with anyone who'll have me? Because being perceived as good doesn't feel nearly as important to me anymore as feeling good?

Let me tell you so no one has to guess.

I'm a queen when I'm dancing under disco balls. A crybaby when it's cold out. I use condoms, but, when I'm in relationships, I sometimes don't. Doctors have told me this is still risky. Men lie. Men cheat. I'm supposed to know better than to not use protection, even with people I love. I'm supposed to know better than to be afraid of HIV, because perpetuating terror would be to betray the people I love who have it. Somewhere in between is what I do know: Sex can be fun if we let it. Strangers will define us if we let them. And what I do: Put on a cute pair of underwear. Wait for my phone to buzz. Play the game. The game is hope.

Cool Mom

"I guess I'm lucky" is what I've started telling people, usually after they hear me laughing with her on the phone, or if I mention something sweet she's done recently, like pay forty dollars to send me a care package of cheese. "I got one of the good ones."

"Have you and your mom always been so cool?" they—friends, coworkers, dates—ask, and I know that by *cool* they don't mean that we smoke weed together wearing matching leather jackets.

I would resent the question—just like I would resent when straight friends invite me to their family's Thanksgiving dinners, assuming I have nowhere else to be—but I understand where it comes from. I know all too many queer people who've been disowned and who scramble every holiday to make plans. It's why gay bars are open year-round. I also know that the reason I get asked is because, even as queer people become more visible, it's still unusual for us to have supportive parents. Which is why every November, it's practically good manners for straight people to assume our relatives don't love us. That's the part I resent, not the generosity of friends, not the question about coolness, but the assumption that I was a difficult son to love. I resent it because it's right.

Just like me, for a long time my mother didn't know what it meant to be gay. In her hometown in Nicaragua, where homosexuality was illegal until 2008, there were none of us out in the open. When she immigrated to Miami in the eighties, the gay scene she encountered was riddled with shame and stigma as thousands of queer people fell to AIDS. I knew, when I came out to her in high school, that what she heard was that I was throwing my life away. There wasn't anyone to tell her it could mean anything else. No one but me, even if I didn't know much more either. Because of that, for much of my life I was on guard against all other queer people. If Mom and I walked by one at the mall, my initial thrill at seeing a gay man out in the open was cut short by the thought: I hope they don't do anything *too gay*.

Whatever she saw in them, I was certain, she would look for in me, as a clue for how I might turn out. *It's nice to see you*, I selfishly wanted to tell them, *but please get away from us*.

Please get away from us because I love my mom, and I don't want her to stop loving me. Because if she sees you wearing those fabulous hoop earrings, those painted-on jeans, sucking down that Frappuccino like that straw should be hanging out of a zipper, she'll start looking at me more closely. Please get away and I'll see you later at Parliament House, is that all right?

It's not you, gorgeous, it's me . . . and my mom. We're not ready yet.

I remember scenes from those years in fragments: Sneaking into her room while she was at work and finding that she'd hid my skinny jeans under her mattress. The tense silences when an aunt or uncle made a comment about me having a girlfriend. The afternoon Mom tackled my locked door to ask, for the thousandth time, if I was still a faggot.

But there's no ideal scene that encapsulates what made things get better. It's not like we were at dinner one day and she lifted her eyes from her plate, stared deeply into a point in the distance, and said, "We're good now." If I really had to guess, it happened sometime after I left her house, when I stopped depending on her for a roof and three meals a day. Once I became self-reliant, I was able to negotiate the terms of our relationship from a place of safety. If she wanted me in her life, she would have to take me as I was. So many of us come out before we get the chance to do that, to stand on our own and figure out who we are for ourselves. We grope through our queerness blindly, hoping our terrified and ill-prepared parents will lead us in the right direction—like they would know any better, like they're not just as lost. It would be nice if we gave ourselves more time before coming out, yet I know that in the moment it feels as if we have no choice but to say it, how badly we need to be reassured. *I'm gay*, we tell the people we love, and as usual, what we don't ask is the question we want answered the most: Is that okay?

For me, the complicated truth is that it wasn't, and then it wasn't a little less, and now it is. But that's not what people want to hear. It's impolite to unload your messy history on someone. So as not to be rude, I say, "I guess I'm lucky," instead of the version that makes room for our flawed relationship: "I'm lucky I was able to leave home, find myself, and become confident enough in who I am that I don't need my mom to accept me. But she does, so she's cool."

We talk on the phone at least once a week. I tell her I'm good. I promise her she doesn't have to worry about me paying rent. I tell her enough about me that she knows it is okay, that being gay doesn't mean what it used to, even if it does. We are still dying of diseases, from bullets. But I also have friends who are happy to take me in over the holidays, just in case.

"Do you know how lucky you are?" I like to remind her every now and then. "I could be like cousin you-know-who, selling radios out my trunk for beer money. I never ask you for help with bills. I'm not out here acting crazy."

"Yeah, yeah," she says and laughs.

"Seriously," I tell her. "I'm basically perfect."

I can almost hear her rolling her eyes on the other end of the line. "Ha!" she says. "Perfect. Well, you got that from me."

I Love San Francisco

The same day I received my acceptance email into the writing program in SoCal, my soon-to-be roommate Bernie, who was working as a journalist for a newspaper in Chile, received hers. She ran out of her office toward the breakroom, where her fiancé, Boris, a journalist for the same newspaper, was making coffee, threw herself into his arms, and told him, well, the news. He jumped up and down. They did that linking-hands-and-spinning-around-really-fast thing. "We're going to California!" she screamed. "I like the Beach Boys!" he answered. Two weeks later they got married in their backyard. A few months after that, we were all sharing a house in Riverside.

At least that's how I imagine it happened. The less cinematic truth—that Bernie took a screengrab of her acceptance letter and told him over WhatsApp—didn't match the deeply-in-love couple I knew in real life. Every morning Boris scurried around our tiny kitchen fixing Bernie cheese and toast and arranging it on a tray with a hand-rolled cigarette and a cup of coffee before taking it upstairs to her in bed. Not long after, the sound of him strumming her a song on the guitar slipped out from beneath their closed bedroom door. From my seat on the couch, I listened to his serenades, feeling like a serial killer who'd accidentally stumbled into a rom-com. Their little kisses. Their matching stick-and-poke tattoos. Their adorable names that sounded like they came packaged in a gift set. I had plenty of reasons to spray Windex in their bottles of pisco. What stopped me was that sometimes Bernie and Boris invited me to their bedroom to have cheese and toast with them, a gesture so kind my bitterness evaporated and I couldn't help but become their friend. First out of necessity, since I knew no one else in Riverside and they were always just *up there*. Then out of an alliance forged by Bernie and me being among the very few Latinx students in most of our graduate seminars.

Over breakfast we showed Boris the feedback our predominantly white classmates gave us, not sure whether to roll our eyes or scream. On a story of mine, about missing my grandmother's funeral in Nicaragua: *Can you mention what kind of food they sell at McDonald's there? I went to Japan once and they had weird stuff. Would help me get a better taste of your culture.* On one of Bernie's, the single note a woman gave her on an essay about the slaughtering of the Mapuche people indigenous to Chile: *Please remember to include page numbers.*

When Boris moved to pick up our dishes, we threw fits like children: Five more minutes. Please. We're sick. We can't go to school today. It was true. The air in the city was so polluted from brush fires and smog we often received texts from the government warning us to stay indoors, like there was anything out there to tempt us. A block from our place was a grocery store I avoided for personal reasons. Beyond that, a Starbucks, which was convenient but hard to summon excitement over. Five more minutes, then we'd leave for class. We splashed water on our faces, dragged ourselves downstairs, sat on the front steps. Five more minutes to pretend we didn't sign up for this, that no one existed but us. A little more time to answer the question a man asked Boris two years earlier, shortly after their plane touched ground on this country.

As Boris tells it, he and Bernie were at an airport in Texas, waiting to transfer to the second plane that would complete their trip from Chile to California, when out of nowhere Boris was seized from the immigration line by armed men in uniform. Bernie stood frozen in panic. How was it possible that barely an hour into their adventure he could already be in trouble? Why were they taking him? What if he couldn't defend himself? What the fuck was happening?

This: inside a dim, windowless room decorated only with a portrait of Barack Obama, an officer repeatedly asked Boris, "Why did you come to the United States?" Boris couldn't think of what to say, even if he had spoken English well enough to say it. Certainly being a Beach Boys fan wouldn't have satisfied the man, who'd just dismissed the answer "To work?" by reminding him he was not eligible to get a job with his spousal visa. Boris stared at his reflection in the metal table, unsure what other excuse to give for his presence, certain that he'd be separated from Bernie, sent right back to Chile, and never know why. Moments before their connecting flight to Riverside took off, he was released without any explanation.

But so was the question, which went on to follow Boris out of Texas, to Riverside, to our house, where it haunted his closest loved one, Bernie, like a ghost with unfinished business. When it dawned on her that she would have to support them with her measly $1,700-per-month student stipend: Why did you come to the United States? When a prominent editor broke it to her that her manuscript, a book about the Augusto Pinochet dictatorship in Chile and the ripples it left on the global south, would never get published "because Americans don't care about what happens in other places": Why did you come to the United States? When it first appeared that the election was tampered with, when news of mass shootings grew dull, when our rent unexpectedly doubled so Boris was forced to take the only job he could get—playing backup horn in a ska band he found on Craigslist. Back home they had their families, successful careers, house plants. Why leave that? To make a hundred bucks a month entertaining wasted sorority girls in cantinas across Pomona? To write a book that apparently no one here would care to read?

"I thought it'd be different," Bernie said one morning. As usual, we were sitting on the front steps of our house, the last red rays of sunrise washing over our miserable faces cradled in our hands. Next to her, Boris nodded and picked at a loose thread on our welcome mat. By then, the question haunted all of us. My answer was the same: I thought it'd be different. I'd hoped moving to a progressive state like California would be a breath of fresh air after living in Florida for over two decades, but so far all I'd accomplished in Riverside was getting an STD from the grocery store checkout guy and almost seeing RuPaul. As for the fresh air I'd sought, regular emergency texts from the government told me it was toxic.

Shortly after Trump was sworn into office, on my walk to school a man yelled "Go back to your country!" at me out of his pickup truck. If not surprised, I'd been shaken then, but after the immediate threat faded, truthfully it didn't seem like such a crazy idea to go home. In a few months Bernie and Boris planned to return to Chile. I would have been happy to go if I had another place to go to. Nicaragua was in the midst of a violent democratic struggle, and going back to my mom's house in Orlando would have been an admission that I couldn't make it on my own, again. Resigned to staying in California, I didn't make plans beyond getting another welcome mat. In the meantime, Bernie, Boris, and I lingered in our doorway, hoping to shroud our memories with nostalgia, the way a silk handkerchief over a lamp can change the tone of a dreary room.

We laughed about the rats that wrestled all night in our

cupboards, the three busted burners on the stove, the washing machine that stained a quarter of our clothes. About the time our landlord came over for a routine visit, and Bernie, showing her around, proudly told her, "We love it here. It is not perfect, but it is our . . . home."

"Can you believe I said that? Our *home?*" She rested her head on Boris's chest and giggled despairingly. "This place sucks."

Boris rubbed her arm.

The one redeeming fact was that they'd gotten to reconnect with long-lost relatives. Through Facebook Bernie found a cousin who lived in San Francisco, and he'd offered us an open invitation to stay at his place whenever we wished. Now that our graduate program was almost over and we were on winter break, Bernie proposed we take a farewell trip there.

I clung to the idea at once, as if it'd been my own, and *I* was the one with the cousin with an apartment in the place where I'd always wanted to live. For as long as I can remember, San Francisco has been my Break in Case of Emergency city, a bunker I'd always figured I could run to if I needed it. Some people played "What would you do if there was a zombie outbreak?" I played "Where would you go if it became illegal to be gay?" The United States wasn't rounding us up for holding hands yet, but it did recently elect a vice president who publicly supported electroshock therapy, transgender children were fighting for their right to use the bathroom in schools, and there was a building in my hometown that I couldn't drive by without my heart racing.

"How soon can we go?" I asked.

Boris's band had a few performances scheduled that week, and Bernie needed to take care of some end-of-the-semester obligations. I wanted to spend a few days there alone, so we agreed that I should leave right away. They would join me New Year's Eve, and we'd cross into January with the same thrill we'd had the day we first found out we were moving to California, when there were no bad memories to shroud, only light, and everything it touched looked good.

Stepping out of the cramped Greyhound that carried me into San Francisco, I lowered my eyes to my cell phone and tried to pinpoint where I stood on the map displayed on my GPS, though I could already feel the answer buzzing in my fingertips. I was exactly where I needed to be. My own country. The proof was everywhere. In the curvy, zigzagging roads, obviously designed by one of my limp-wristed ancestors. In the accessible public transit, a thoughtful precaution for bottoms who can't drive. Even the trash littering the bus stop was gay. Granola bar wrappers and cigarette butts. Artifacts, I instantly recognized, left behind by a lesbian reeling after a breakup.

Beside me on the sidewalk a fellow passenger dug through her luggage and pulled out a thick wool sweater. Suddenly I understood my fingertips weren't buzzing because I was standing on holy land. Duh, they were going numb. It'd been a month of crop-top weather in Riverside, but the temperature here was below sixty. My bus clothes—a baggy T-shirt and track pants—were useless against the cold. So were the cut-off jean shorts and sandals in my book bag. I typed "thrift store" into my GPS and watched several results pop up in a neighborhood called Haight-Ashbury.

By the time I arrived, afternoon was already fading into dusk. I made my way through the packed sidewalk teeming with men draped in turquoise jewelry and bald women wearing head-to-toe hemp, teenagers with dangly crucifix earrings weaving between them on longboards. There was something strange about everyone, something I wasn't used to. I didn't see a sad face, not a single cheek streaked with mascara. What kind of gays were these? The ones I knew didn't smile so much. At our happiest, we were brooding out of car windows.

I tried not to indulge my skepticism and let the current push me forward. Gradually the crowd thinned out, and in the distance a small clearing opened. In it, a man with big, bushy eyebrows and a crooked nose leaned against a light post, the pages of the book in his hand fluttering in the breeze. I don't know if it was because he was alone or because I was in San Francisco, but I stopped and pictured the two of us in bed, my legs wrapped around his hairy thighs; his faint, nasal snore; the familiar thirst I felt after watching even the worst Jennifer Lopez movie. Because, sure, anywhere else, the odds of meeting someone by tripping on a sewer grate were low. That they'd be gay, too, impossible. But here, in the queerest city in the United States, the possibility of falling in love with someone I met on the street blossomed before me.

Still, I'd had enough straight dudes blow up in my face to know to be careful before flirting with a stranger, that even a "hey" takes delicate calibration, an assessment of their politics, adjustments to minimize the probability that they'll kill me, or, worse, mumble "Oh no, sorry, um . . . no, I'm not . . ." under their breath. Just in case, I studied the man from afar, searching for clues to his potential queerness. Before gay bars, before dating apps and the internet, isn't that how we met? Cruising? Weren't we supposed to have hidden senses to help us figure out who it's okay to approach, like how trees in forests use their roots to communicate with each other? I extended mine. He was drinking an iced coffee in the winter (a good start) and had dark circles under his eyes (perfect for brooding), and the hems of his jeans were cuffed (could go either way). As I added and subtracted those queer signifiers, I glanced down at my track pants and brushed the lint off the hole in my crotch where I'd dropped a lit joint that morning. Compared to everyone else walking by, I looked like my sexuality was ripping bongs.

I wondered: If he gave me a once-over, would he know I was gay? The idea that he might *not* threw me. Only the opposite had ever been true. I was almost always too femme, too clockable. I'm scrawny. I bounce when I walk. I carry my phone in my hand like a little coin purse. I fit neatly into the popular definition of what gay men look like. It's risky to be easily identifiable, which is why I primarily stick to places where I have backup. Bars. Around friends. In the Haight, however, everyone was dressed as if they were headed off to Pride.

Yet instead of filling me with hope about a future where we're all free to express ourselves, I could only think of all the mornings my more feminine-presenting friends and I wasted staring into our closets, deciding whether we wanted to have a good day or bad day. Maybe that was why all the smiling here made me uncomfortable. I wouldn't have minded if I knew all these people were gay, but statistically not even half were; I wasn't even sure about the one person I was interested in. Their happiness flaunted what I could never have in Riverside and Orlando, where I was too busy looking over my shoulder to enjoy wearing anything cute. It wasn't fair for them to get to experiment with fashion so brazenly, not when queer people elsewhere in the country had to wipe off their nail polish before heading to job interviews. If anyone was going to look gay, I thought, it should be one of *us*.

I dipped into the nearest thrift store, throwing away any sense of caution, and emerged an hour later wearing an itchy baby-blue sweater that barely covered my belly button, camo-print pants, and a pink, checkered beret. The clothes were out of my budget and not that warm, but they made me feel something: undeniable, militant, like a high-risk homosexual.

I scanned the sidewalk for my potential boyfriend and/or murderer, finally prepared to say hello. Night had fallen on the block since I'd entered the store. It was nearly empty now except for a few stragglers. Gold light from the streetlamp illuminated the patch of concrete where he'd been. I'd taken too long. He was gone.

All at once, as I stood there alone, my chest deflated, reality flooded back in. I was freezing, on my own, with not a lot of money and no friends nearby. I sat down on a bench and ordered a cab, hoping it would come quick. Dressed this way, it wasn't safe to be on some street corner, making myself known.

Half an hour later the driver pulled into a neighborhood that was quaint in that deceptive way only people descended from evil can afford in big cities. No trash, no bumper stickers on the backs of any cars. Ivy bloomed along the front steps of the townhouse we pulled up to like the train of a gown, wrapping around an elegant archway shielding a tobacco-colored door fitted with a brass lion's head knocker.

"This the one?" he asked, sounding a little too impressed. I would have been upset, but even I could admit that the kind of person who lived here didn't carry a backpack with a marijuana-leaf patch.

"Yeah," I couldn't resist the urge to say. "This is me."

It wasn't a total lie. Bernie's cousin Javi and his five roommates, all college students, were out of town on holiday break. Until New Year's, this place was all mine.

I stepped out of the cab and pretended to act casual as I lifted potted plants in search of the spare key. I kept pretending as I pushed through the front door and was greeted by dented energy-drink cans scattered along the dark, narrow staircase leading up to the second floor. It had to be one of the other tenants, I told myself, kicking the cans aside as I climbed the steps.

Inside Javi's apartment, a musty hallway with bedrooms branching off on either side led me to the kitchen/living room, where I found a Post-it note stuck to a Ping-Pong table with the message "Mi casa es su casa . . ." An open bag of chips lay tipped over on its side. Rows of ants marched their dinner down one of the table's legs, disappearing into cracks in the wood floor.

The roughly seven hundred dollars a month Bernie told me each roommate paid for rent was beginning to seem like less of a steal than I'd thought. I set my bags down on a sectional couch that presided over DIY pizza-box furniture. In response it coughed out a small cloud of dust, as if clearing its throat before apologizing. *Our bad, dude, we were expecting stoner-you from the Greyhound, not this bougie queen in a floppy hat.*

I peeked into Javi's room, praying that at least his personal space would be clean, and discovered that his so-called personal space was split into two equal parts with a bamboo privacy screen to allow him to share it with someone else. I left it for Bernie and Boris, since they were family, and moved on to the other rooms. The next one over was also shared. In the farthest corner, a condom lay unfurled on the ground like a discarded snakeskin. The third room had one of those magnifying mirrors that show you extreme close-ups of your pores. As far as I was concerned, both were equally uninhabitable. Back at the beginning of the hallway, the final door opened into a closet just barely containing a twin-sized mattress. A fire escape looked out onto the tree-lined street. Neatly arranged along the window frame were several precious stones, a pack of matchsticks, and a postcard from Argentina. I worried briefly that my moving in would displace a tragic, heartbroken elf, but I followed Javi's instructions and made myself at home.

Sprawled out on the tiny bed that night, I scrolled through Grindr and took sips from one of the energy drinks I found in the fridge while trying in vain to tidy up—washing the dishes clogged the sink, the mop strings were stiffer than the floor, and their only cleaning solution was a leaky bottle of two-in-one shampoo/conditioner stashed under the sink. I understood why the elf was depressed. On Grindr, I sought out distraction. Though I couldn't find the man from the Haight, it was satisfying to see my square profile arranged neatly next to thousands of others, whereas in Riverside I could fit all the queer people into a conference call. Slowly messages began to come in. A man five hundred feet away asked if he could spend the night. Others were interested in smoking a little, messing around. I blushed, thinking of what my life here would be like. Then, one by one, I wrote back no, sorry, I couldn't. It'd be rude to invite people over without Javi's permission, and he had already been so generous: not only did he lend us his apartment, he also left behind a bottle of champagne as a New Year's gift. Despite his hospitality, I couldn't help resenting him for having what I didn't. This apartment was no more to him than a frat house, whereas I spent half my life brooding out of car windows, dreaming of the day I'd make it here.

I took a NyQuil. Throughout the night the sound of incoming messages pierced my sleep, waking me with delight at the thought that I'd finally made it. Barely a second later I'd push my phone away, remembering I was lying on someone else's bed.

Ask Google what you should do when you get to San Francisco, and you will find hundreds of lists offering you urgent suggestions. You most definitely have to walk across the Golden Gate Bridge, and while you're there you'd be a fool not to follow that with a leisurely stroll through Golden Gate Park. You can't miss hiking up one of the city's infamous hills, which pairs perfectly with a ride back down on a historic cable car. For an authentic local experience, rent a bike. At some point you should also take a ferry to Alcatraz, a Swedish lady seriously wrote on her blog. All of these options are presented with the implicit understanding that at the end of the hike or bus or boat trip you will find something great, because everywhere in San Francisco is great. All you need to do is go outside to experience this greatness for yourself.

So that was my plan, I decided when I woke up the

following morning. Forget the apartment. Commute to greatness. Tackle the city like a white woman going to prison. The Castro seemed like the perfect place to start. I knew almost nothing about the neighborhood other than that it was where Harvey Milk used to operate a camera store and that it's considered the heart of gay San Francisco. Perhaps I could have bothered to research it more, but it was the *idea* of a haven for queer people, not seeing a blueprint of it, that had sustained me on nights when I needed to believe there was somewhere out there that belonged to us. I stole another energy drink from the fridge and left the apartment jittery.

Walking, I figured, would give me the best chance of stumbling upon a hidden gem. I expected San Francisco would be mostly gentrified, but I figured there still had to be pockets of what it used to be, a McDonald's with culturally specific menu offerings, their ground beef marinated in poppers. My journey took me past a Starbucks, and a chain grocery store, and a boutique that sold very tall, very beige candles. Just as I was beginning to lose hope, a seedy-looking bar with drawn blinds and teddy bear stickers plastered to the windows caught my eye down the street. I hurried over, only to find out it was a daycare.

After a while my GPS signaled that I had finally reached the Castro. I stared at my blue dot on the map. I looked to my left at a Bank of America, to my right at a swarm of people cutting across a rainbow-painted crosswalk. Then I waited.

For what, it's hard to say. Something. Wasn't something supposed to happen?

Something like at the end of zombie movies, when the road-weary protagonist arrives at the sanctuary he was never sure existed beyond word of mouth, and the gates open, and he discovers that on the other side is his family, plus all the people who helped him get there: Angel and Miguel and Arturo and Polylust and Hector and my mother.

Or something like a feeling. Like the one you get listening to "Over the Rainbow." Like maybe you haven't heard enough stories about queer people where they don't die, but for an instant it feels possible there might be a graceful arc to a life like yours.

Something that would allow me to subvert the advice shouted by the man from his car, because—ha!—look: I did go back to my country, and it was great!

But of course nothing did. What happened was I slid my phone into my pocket and headed in the same direction as everyone else, not quite sure where I was going or why.

Eventually I stopped at a bakery where a group of girls were taking selfies with their novelty penis-shaped cookies. The woman behind the counter noticed the worn paperback copy of *Running with Scissors* in my hands and suggested I check out a queer bookstore a few doors down if I had time, which I had so, so much of. There, I wandered around flipping through books about queer history, about *gay dining*, and gasped when I saw a magazine with a cover of two men kissing underneath a blue neon sign that spelled Pulse. The sign seemed, in my desperation to find meaning in this trip, like *a sign*. I opened the magazine. Skimmed it front to back twice. There was no mention of the club. The sign was just a sign, nothing more, just like, years later, there was no more sense to those completely preventable murders. The magazine sent me running to the nearest gay bar, as the thought of Pulse always did. I ordered a fifteen-dollar martini. I stood beneath very tall, very beige people while porn played on television monitors. I nodded along to the new Lady Gaga song playing on the stereo.

Girl, it was all right.

The Castro was just all right.

On the way home I passed the Starbucks and the grocery store and the daycare again, annoyed with myself for not being any different than Javi and his roommates, who treated San Francisco as if it were nowhere special. I'd spent so much of my life trying to be palatable, trying to stay safe, and now I was in a city where survival wasn't my number one priority, but I didn't know what to do with myself. Eat gay cookies? Read gay books? Listen to Lady Gaga? Those things were fun, but were they all the last two decades of my life had been leading up to? Was this really everything that was waiting for me, for us, at the end of the rainbow?

There used to be a place for queer people. After a few more days of exploring, I went to what was left of it: a faded blue building on the corner of Turk and Taylor Streets in the

Tenderloin district, the former site of Gene Compton's all-night cafeteria.

In the summer of 1966, when it was still around, it was the place to go for people who had nowhere else. Drag queens, trans women, girly-boys; for some, the lines were still blurry then. They met at the diner at the end of most nights, paying for their sixty-cent coffee with whatever cash they earned from walking the street doing sex work or performing in cabaret shows. Outside Compton's the rest of the city wanted nothing to do with them, effectively granting the girls the fifty square blocks of the Tenderloin to roam but only that: résumés handed in to employers elsewhere were balled up and thrown in the trash, tenant applications slid to the bottom of the pile. A news report from that time describes the area as a "marketplace of vice, degradation, and human misery." Inside Compton's there were eggs, greasy slices of bacon, glasses of neon-tinted orange juice, though the girls I've read about usually stuck to coffee.

The seats by the windows were especially popular. There they could show off their outfits. Floral-print dresses cut a few inches above the knee, silk handkerchiefs tied into bows around their necks. They crossed their smooth legs and trailed their manicured fingers around the rims of their mugs, blowing kisses at the hustlers coming out of the bathhouse or porn theater next door, the Hells Angels who lined their bikes down the block to party. The girls could gossip for hours. Laugh. Check in with each other. They pushed their mugs to the edge of their tables for more. Three years before the Stonewall riots in New York, which would erase them from the general LGBT consciousness, every night was like this.

One night a waitress glided through a full house. *It's an art*, she might have muttered to herself, pouring fresh coffee into a waiting cup. This job. Another refill. Feet swollen like a ballerina's. When a police unit walked in. Nothing unusual. Every night was like this. *IDs*, they asked the girls. If the "boys" on the cards didn't match what they saw in front of them, they could take them in. It was a crime: the dresses, silk handkerchiefs. "Female impersonation."

But this night was not like every night. Something happened.

Instead of letting the cops haul them to jail again, the girls said, "Enough." Enough of these inhumane arrests. Of being told who they were. One drew her coffee mug close to her chest and, when a cop put his hands on her, threw her hot drink in his face. Other trans women, drag queens, girly-boys joined in, unleashing their pent-up frustration by shattering the windows with salt shakers, beating the other officers with their handbags. When management threw them out, they rioted in the streets, demanding an end to the harassment, trashing a cop car, and setting a news stand on fire.

Over half a century later, I can only imagine how bittersweet the flames tasted on their faces, the question that must have crossed their minds as they tore apart one of the few places they had before they let it be taken from them: Now where are we going to go?

A question that still haunts the building, which has since been converted into a transitional facility for recently released inmates and is run by a private prison corporation.

A question that stirred up a memory I'd buried a long time ago, of when I was thirteen years old, on the balcony of my uncle's house in Nicaragua, looking down at a group of women just like the women from Compton's.

"¡Oye, lindo!" one of them had said. Hello, beautiful.

Back then I wondered why she'd felt comfortable speaking to me, considering that almost any other child would have run away. In retrospect I'm certain it had nothing to do with the sound of my voice or my "queer clothes." She must have seen me watching her. How mesmerized I'd been by her stilettos and tight dress, the calmness and inner poise she exuded as she leaned into the car windows of men who pulled over. Now I think she spoke to me because, unlike those men who sped off when they realized who she was, I stayed. That's what cruising is, in its simplest form. Looking. Staying. She spoke to me because she knew I would listen.

Though I'd been terrified to see a part of myself reflected in her—a woman walking what was clearly a dangerous line—that chance meeting was what saved me from believing the stories about queer people that made us all out to seem degraded or miserable or any other word meant to reduce our existences to cautionary tales. I saw someone laughing with her girlfriends, wearing a cute outfit, someone more than surviving. She was alive.

Surely, I thought, heading back to Javi's apartment from

Compton's, I should be satisfied that I didn't have to fight like the women at the cafeteria did, or hide as I'd had to when I was thirteen. Surely it should be enough to be here, in a city the boy I was back then could only dream of. And yet I wanted more. I expected more. Queer people give up so much to be who we are, risking our lives, our families, our jobs, our sanity. I didn't regret coming out of the closet, but if someone were to ask me, "For what? Was it worth it?" I don't know what I would have told them. San Francisco wasn't our reward. It was just another place. Behind thick clouds of fog, the city played peekaboo, briefly revealing itself, then fading out, like a Polaroid in reverse.

"What about this?" Bernie asked Boris and me the night they arrived. She plopped down between us on the living room couch, where Boris had been teaching me to roll a blunt with a wooden contraption, and showed us the New Year's party flier Javi had messaged her. On it, a cartoon Drake showered Cardi B in dollar bills. "It's only a few blocks away. Could be cool."

"All right," I said, having no doubt the club would be just that. We'd spent the hours since they got off the bus exploring the same places in the city I had gone to alone, and still San Francisco hadn't answered the questions that'd been nagging me since I visited Compton's.

But it was New Year's, and before I knew it Bernie and Boris would be in Chile again, so I put my questions aside and resigned myself to having a good time. Besides, even if the city didn't deliver a cinematic happy ending, I was a writer, months away from holding a master's degree, with people I liked and who liked me. I couldn't complain.

Boris handed me the finished blunt, leapt to his feet, and darted over to his laptop on the Ping-Pong table, pressing play on a reggaeton track that made Bernie and me clap our hands over our laughing mouths and get up too. We pulled out the bottle of champagne Javi left us in the fridge while Boris threw open the windows, the frosty night air rushing inside. Bernie popped the cork and screamed, "We're in San Francisco!" I wanted to be as excited as she was, so I screamed it after her, then bent over to catch the foam dripping from the bottle's mouth with my tongue. We danced around the living room pretending no one existed but us.

"You know what sucks the most about this country?" Bernie asked when the bottle was half empty.

I had no idea.

"Your bread," she said. "You have no bread culture here."

"¡Sí, po!" Boris yelled from his makeshift DJ booth. "¡El pan de aquí es *lo más* pésimo!"

I took their word for it. It was reassuring, actually, to know that the worst thing about the United States was our bread, at least for now. Tomorrow we might remember everything else. Tonight we refilled our coffee mugs with the last of the champagne and toasted to better toast.

Before heading to the club, we split up to change clothes. A few minutes later we met up in the kitchen, me in my high-risk homosexual outfit, Boris wearing a baggy corduroy suit. Beside him, Bernie applied red lipstick to go with her vampy black dress. "That's what you're wearing?" she looked up at me from her compact mirror and cocked an eyebrow.

"We're in San Francisco!" I reminded her.

I should have taken her warning. At the club I found out where all the straight-looking straight people in the city had been hiding—a discovery I first became aware of when I saw that there was a line out the door thirty people deep, all the women in bodycon dresses, all the men in button-ups and boat shoes. Almost none of the gay clubs I'd ever been to had had a line. There was always room. You could always get in. I worried I might not, but Bernie linked her arm in mine, and an hour before midnight the bouncer let the three of us through.

I slid my beret into my pocket and tried not to think about how much I stood out. Bernie and Boris made me feel like less of an outsider. The combination of my looking extra as hell and them not knowing most of the English songs playing brought us closer together. We sipped fizzy drinks under a constellation of disco balls until the DJ announced there were ten seconds left in the year. The countdown began. Everyone who'd brought a date grabbed them by the hands. Everyone who didn't found someone quick. On impulse, I looked all over—just in case—but no one had magically appeared to give me a rom-com ending, not even in San Francisco. Confetti rained from the ceiling as the couples around me kissed. I was just tipsy enough to not feel too bummed listening to the celebratory trumpet music swelling in the room, just buzzed enough for the world to briefly shift into slow motion as I stood there alone. Next to me, Boris held on to Bernie, his forehead pressed to hers like she was worth all the bad bread he'd put up with for the last two years, and I knew she was the answer to "Why did you come to the United States?"

Looking at them it finally clicked why San Francisco had merely been all right. I appreciated that there was more safety and opportunity for queer people here, the legacy of the trans women of color who, fighting for themselves, taught me not to accept anything less than what I deserved. The existence of a city where the probability that someone will yell a slur at you is low is undeniable progress. But it's not *great*. It's not enough.

Kids questioning whether to come out aren't swayed by the hope that someday they will be tolerated. I wasn't. I didn't do it to be "brave," or to inspire. I don't think the women at Compton's did either. For much of my childhood, I didn't even really know what it meant to be gay. Don't get me wrong, I understood it had something to do with the tingling in my arms when my best friend's thigh brushed against mine on the school bus, but more urgent to me then were what Mom's reaction would be, whether Hector would hate me, if I'd be kicked out of my house. That's how I defined queerness: consequences. There was no joy in the word, nothing happy about it. It wasn't until sophomore year of high school that I met a boy who made me realize there were benefits too. That's what I wanted from The Castro: something to remind me of the good things, things worth fighting for. Like two of my best friends kissing, like love.

Back in the depressed little elf's bedroom that night, I climbed out onto the fire escape to give Bernie and Boris privacy inside. The heavy fog deadened the bright lights of the city, outlining the world in silver. I brought my knees to my chest and again thought of who I used to be all those years ago, how desperately I'd wanted to go downstairs and talk to the women, ask them whether it was worth it. For countless closeted people, it isn't. You can lose so much by coming out. But if you are lucky there is so much to be gained.

Worth, like every great thing, is made up of many small ones. It was worth it when kissing Angel, wrapped up in the red velvet curtain during drama rehearsal, and when I was with all those other men who pulled me into cars and beds and dance floors to show me something new. It's worth it when I put on clothes I like, instead of settling for clothes that will make people look through me. It's worth it when I think of the friends I would have never been introduced to, the bonds with my mother and my brother that were earned, the fact queers being barred from institutions like marriage and religion means we get to define what relationships and spirituality mean for ourselves. It's worth it when I add up all the grueling hours I don't have to spend with people, some of them relatives, who don't know how to love me and who I don't want to waste my life teaching. It might not always be worth it, but it was in the chilly early hours of the new year, as I snuck downstairs to go find a gay bar, a drag show, and maybe someone to have cheese and toast with in the morning, guided by the same instinct I had at thirteen, and the only thing I was certain of right then.

What you do when you're not afraid anymore is the same thing you do when you are: keep going.

Acknowledgments

Before I wrote a word in these pages, I was just a scared kid on my uncle's balcony in Nicaragua. I know they'll probably never see this, but I can't imagine this book would exist if I hadn't met those women who showed me what life could be, so to them I say: thank you.

The same goes for all the courageous activists and artists who inspire me every day. Thank you, Susan Stryker, for your research on the riot at Gene Compton's Cafeteria. Thank you, Marsha P. Johnson and Sylvia Rivera, for being loud and beautiful. Thank you, Wilson Cruz, for giving me something to look forward to on television. Thank you, Janet Mock, for sharing your truth in your brilliant memoirs. Thank you, Walter Mercado, for insisting on hope. Thank you, James Baldwin, for your wisdom. Thank you, Rigoberto González, for writing people and places that look familiar to me. Thank you, Pedro Almodóvar, for all the complex women in your films. Thank you, Darcel Stevens, Jazell Barbie Royale, Sonique, and Shantell D'Marco, for making my Sunday nights at the Parliament House.

I also want to thank some people I wasn't able to put in this book. I promise you it isn't because you weren't important, but because your personalities are so big I couldn't begin to do them justice in such a small amount of space. I could write a book for each one of you alone.

Elyse and Jason, thank you for being so funny and for always welcoming me into your apartment/house/roof, even when I was a little weirdo freak who didn't speak.

Socorro Bendaña, gracias abuelita. Encontré la maña.

Betsy and Vanessa, thank you for making art, which made it feel possible for me to make some too.

Joseph, thank you for keeping me sane and alive during quarantine.

Will, thank you for pushing me to do more than I thought possible.

Marianna, thank you for the Kindle. I told you I wouldn't forget.

Laura, thank you for generously paying to repair my laptop at the last minute, without which I would have quite literally not been able to write this, and especially thank you for watching *Showgirls* with me my first month in California.

People of Polylust not mentioned, thank you for being sexy.

Erika and Sarah and Megan and Ava and Alejandro and Colton and Aidan, thank you for being swamp boys with me.

Bernie and Boris, you're in this book, but an extra thank you. For being my sanctuary in Riverside, introducing me to pisco sours, and not judging my high-risk activity.

Arturo, you're in this book too, but in case I haven't said it enough: girl, I love you.

At UC Riverside: Thank you, Alan, for being the sweetest, smartest friend. Thank you, Ashanti, for the afternoon we sat in the back of the museum laughing. Thank you, Natassja and Chloe, for our depressing lunches. Thank you, Laila Lalami, Susan Straight, Emily Rapp Black, and Goldberry Long, for lending my writing your eyes.

Thank you to the literary magazines that published earlier versions of these stories. "Malcriado" appeared in *Ploughshares* (2019). "There Used to Be a Gay Bar" appeared as "Pulse Nightclub Was My Home" in *Longreads* (2017). "Boy's Club" appeared in *The Rumpus* (2014).

Thank you to the people of Jackson Heights, Queens, and the volunteers at the Love Wins Food Pantry for being the end of the rainbow I'd hoped San Francisco would be.

Thank you to my agent, Danielle Bukowski, for believing in me, for telling me within ten minutes of meeting that you would never ask me to write about trauma, and for selling this book in the middle of a global pandemic.

At Soft Skull Press: thank you to my editor, Sarah Lyn Rogers, for all your thoughtful notes and for insisting I'm not corny. Thank you, Michael Salu, for designing such a joyous cover. Thank you, Wah-Ming Chang, Barrett Briske, Yuka Igarashi, and the rest of team who helped bring this book to life.

Lastly, I want to hold space for the queer people who lost their lives at Pulse. I will think of you and thank you my entire life.

Rest in peace.

Stanley Almodovar III
Amanda L. Alvear
Oscar A. Aracena Montero
Rodolfo Ayala Ayala
Alejandro Barrios Martinez
Martin Benitez Torres
Antonio Davon Brown
Darryl Roman Burt II
Jonathan A. Camuy Vega
Angel L. Candelario-Padro
Simón Adrian Carrillo
  Fernández
Juan Chavez Martinez
Luis Daniel Conde
Cory James Connell
Tevin Eugene Crosby
Franky Jimmy DeJesus
  Velázquez
Deonka Deidra Drayton
Mercedez Marisol Flores
Peter Ommy Gonzalez
  Cruz

Juan Ramon Guerrero
Paul Terrell Henry
Frank Hernandez
Miguel Angel Honorato
Javier Jorge Reyes
Jason Benjamin Josaphat
Eddie Jamoldroy Justice
Anthony Luis Laureano
  Disla
Christopher Andrew
  Leinonen
Brenda Marquez McCool
Jean Carlos Mendez Perez
Akyra Monet Murray
Kimberly Jean Morris
Jean Carlos Nieves
  Rodríguez
Luis Omar Ocasio Capo
Geraldo A. Ortiz Jimenez
Eric Ivan Ortiz-Rivera
Joel Rayon Paniagua
Enrique L. Rios Jr.

Juan Pablo Rivera
Velázquez
Yilmary Rodríguez
Solivan
Christopher Joseph
Sanfeliz
Xavier Emmanuel Serrano-
Rosado

Gilberto Ramon Silva
Menendez
Edward Sotomayor Jr.
Shane Evan Tomlinson
Leroy Valentin Fernandez
Luis Sergio Vielma
Luis Daniel Wilson-Leon
Jerald Arthur Wright

EDGAR GOMEZ is a Florida-born writer with roots in Nicaragua and Puerto Rico. A graduate of University of California, Riverside's MFA program, he is a recipient of the 2018 Marcia McQuern Graduate Award in Nonfiction. His work has been published and anthologized in such outlets as *Popsugar, Longreads, Best Gay Stories, The Rumpus,* and *Ploughshares.* He lives in Queens, New York, where he is saving up for good lotion.